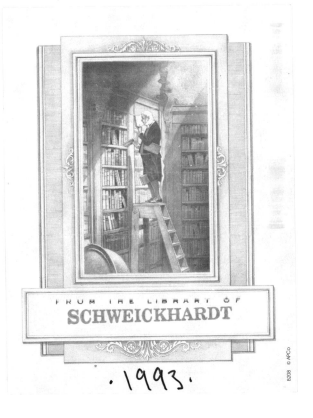

FROM THE LIBRARY OF
SCHWEICKHARDT

·1993·

B208 © APCo

Returning Words to Flesh

RETURNING WORDS TO FLESH

Feminism, Psychoanalysis, AND THE Resurrection of the Body

Naomi R. Goldenberg

BEACON PRESS · BOSTON

Beacon Press
25 Beacon Street
Boston, Massachusetts 02108-2800

Beacon Press books
are published under the auspices of
the Unitarian Universalist Association of
Congregations.

97 96 95 94 93 92 91 90   8 7 6 5 4 3 2 1

Text design by Gwen Frankfeldt

Library of Congress Cataloging-in-Publication Data
Goldenberg, Naomi R.
    Returning words to flesh : feminism, psychoanalysis, and the
resurrection of the body / Naomi R. Goldenberg.
        p.   cm.
    Includes bibliographical references.
    ISBN 0-8070-6738-5
    1. Psychoanalysis and feminism.   2. Body, Human—Psychological
aspects.   I. Title.
B175.4.F45G64 1990
150.19′5′082—dc20   89-46062

For Natalie and Bob

Contents

Contents

Acknowledgments

The ideas I have written about in these essays come out of discussions with several people. Conversations with Geraldine Finn, Donna Jowett, and Caryll Steffens have been my chief source of inspiration, support, and delight over the years I have been working. In addition, talks with Dorothy Austin have been invaluable.

I am grateful to Drs. Dean Eyre, Ann Mully, and Ben Esrock, from whom I have learned about psychoanalysis. My research was also aided by the members of the Ottawa Branch of the Canadian Psychoanalytic Society, who welcomed me as a guest member. Dr. Ahmed Fayek's "Freud Group" was a help to me as well.

I want to thank Joanne Wyckoff, my editor, for her insight and support. And I much appreciate the encouragement I have received from Carol Christ, Bob Fife, and Deborah Gorham. Phyllis Leonardi and Zayn Kassam-Hann were also very helpful.

Gillian Smith shared the last stages of the project with me. Her fine mind and keen sense for the subtleties in language and theory have been a great benefit to the book.

My research was helped by a leave fellowship which the Social Sciences and Humanities Research Council of Canada granted me in 1983–84. I hope that such grants will someday be available to the Canadian academic community once again.

Introduction

I began these essays almost as a meditation on a remark I heard a psychoanalyst make to a colleague (analysts, it seems to me, are often trying to explain to themselves and others just what it is they do). "Psychoanalysis," said this man, "puts you in touch with your body." That's right, I thought, I agree with that. Psychoanalysis is talk that works through the body. I realized that what psychoanalysis was offering me was a connection with emotions and personal history. This connection was something I could sense physically. Previously, only my participation in feminist consciousness-raising groups had shown me that talk could reveal such depths and dimensions in human beings. I realized that for me both psychoanalysis and feminism were revitalizing ways of thinking, which helped me to resist the stultifying atmosphere of the university.

I know I am not alone in feeling that the scope of academic life in North America has narrowed over the past several years.[1] My awareness of this constriction grew gradually as I noticed there were fewer and fewer lectures, conferences, and discussions on campus which could hold my attention for very long. At university events, in former years, I frequently listened to people whose ideas expanded my thinking and inspired me. Now, at similar occasions, I too often hear the hum of the fluorescent lights and feel that rarely is anything being said which matters very much either to the speaker or to the audience.

Since I am one of those who, for better or worse, needs to live within a world of theory and thought, it has become increasingly more challenging to identify ideas which feed me, which keep my mind alive so that I can, from time to time, feed my students. Because life as a university professor no longer presents me with a cornucopia of food for thought, I have had to become better at hunting and gathering—better at finding ways of thinking which can sustain me. I consider the essays in this book as the record of my search for food, for nourishment in the form of ideas which open up the world rather than shut it down.

I have arranged the book thematically to move from statements of what I consider the problem to glimpses of solution. In the first essay, "Apocalypse in Everyday Life: The Cultural Context in Which We Do Theory," and the first two sections, "Readings in Body Language (Mostly Male)" and "Escape from Jung: Psychoanalytic/Feminist Critiques," I discuss how Western life and thought fragments both our bodies and our social relationships. In the last section, "Feminism and Psychoanalysis: Overlaps and Interludes," I explore what I see as the beginning of an answer: the encouraging of sustained conversations and more public concern with memories of personal and collective history.

My work on relationships between body and thought began when I realized that engagement with psychoanalytic and feminist theory was leading me away from the stagnant, overly defined patterns of seeing, working, and living which I describe in "Apocalypse in Everyday Life." I find it strange that, for me, psychoanalytic theory opposes the numbed *Zeitgeist* which permeates academia as well as most other institutions in North America. After all, psychoanalytic papers are often badly written and dry as dust, analytic meetings are tedious, and analysts as a group are very conservative and frequently seem not at all aware of much beyond their consulting rooms or the politics of their profession. The desire to understand why psychoanalysis, like feminism, has had the power to animate and transform me has motivated my writing over the past seven years.

I think that the ability of psychoanalysis to connect us with our bodies lies in the fact that it shows how what we say is profoundly linked to our physical and emotional experience as well as to our history with other people. Within an analysis, language becomes embodied when it resonates with desires, hopes, and fears for past and present. Because interest is focused on the physical, emotional, historical contexts of words, thoughts, and actions, all language is shown to be body language.[2]

In contrast to psychoanalysis, which focuses on the embodiment of individuals, feminism has been more concerned with understanding how the facts of physicality are interpreted within societies. Feminist theory has shown me that we women symbolize the body in much of contemporary culture. The work which we have traditionally been assigned is centered on bodies: feeding, cleaning, comforting, adorning. We represent sensuality itself with our clothing and decoration. Our culture tends to prescribe uniforms for men—suits and clothes that standardize their bodies and make them monochromatic. Women, in contrast, are encouraged to use a range of fabrics, colors, styles, and ornaments. We present ourselves as the varied ones—as the textured, embodied members of the species.

I think that as women we have never been allowed to entertain the illusion that our minds are separate from our bodies, or that we have a public life that is discontinuous with our

3

private selves. Feminist anthropologist Karen Brown once said that no matter what job a woman has, it is she who will always have to know how much milk is in the refrigerator. On a related theme, Christiane Rochefort writes:

> We have a body: university degrees don't obliterate the fact. When [Julia]Kristeva got a prize not long ago, a critic wrote in a so-called liberal newspaper: "She has beautiful legs." We have a physiology: after de Beauvoir's novel *La femme rompue,* the critic of *Le Monde* said, "She's an old woman." He himself was about to die, but he was a man and consequently had no age.[3]

By no means do I find the association of women and body all bad. It is men's refusal to see themselves as bodies that has rendered the equation of women with body confining and oppressive. In fact, their greater awareness of physical and social contingency gives many women a depth and wisdom that men often lack.

Paradoxically, although women and body are so closely linked in contemporary imagination, public culture is largely structured around ideas about male bodies. "On Hockey Sticks and Hopscotch Patsies: Reflections on the Sexuality of Sport" is the first essay I wrote about the public body language of which I was becoming increasingly aware. I began to see that sports could be considered a highly stylized form of speech expressing very particular bodily concerns. The rules of many games are scripts, texts that reflect and glorify maleness. I had fun with this satire. After writing it, however, my mood became more serious. I began to understand that much of the philosophy, psychology, and theology I had studied should also be considered forms of sport which are as ritualized and male-focused as any of the stick sports. Two essays, one on the work of Norman O. Brown, and the other on the concept of identity, elaborate this idea.

4

Looking back on these essays, which appear under the heading "Readings in Body Language (Mostly Male)," I see how angry I have been about the ways in which culture built around an idealized male body has circumscribed my life as a woman. By disturbing that hegemony, by allowing other bodies more space for their own cultural expressions, I think feminism could enlarge everyone's field of play.

In the section called "Escape from Jung," I argue that we need to read Jung from what could be called a psychoanalytic/feminist perspective. Like many theorists, Jung could not see how his work was rooted in the contingency of his own life. He developed a psychological/religious system in which thought itself is seen as disembodied, as arising from "archetypes"—that is, from forces wholly outside any human context. Since Jungian psychology is a form of patriarchal religion within which I once lived and worked, understanding the limitations of that system has been particularly important to me. My critique aims to dismantle Jung's thought by embodying it—by linking his ideas to his life and social circumstances. I hope that feminists who are interested in other thinkers will find such an approach useful.

In all the essays, the parallels between psychoanalysis and feminism have been of greater interest to me than the differences. In the essays in the last section, "Psychoanalysis and Feminism: Overlaps and Interludes," I concentrate on the implications of two parallels between these two bodies of theory: namely, that both employ a talking cure, and that both take childhood and sexuality as central subjects. These themes, as I will explain, give feminism and psychoanalysis power to remind us of what Adrienne Rich has referred to as the "corporeal ground of our intelligence."

All the essays discuss the need to understand how thought is always embodied, that is, always contingent on human cir-

5

cumstance and subjectivity. By calling this book, *Returning Words to Flesh: Feminism, Psychoanalysis, and the Resurrection of the Body*, I am deliberately using religious language to describe my project. I like the sound of this title because for me it says two very important things.

First, it points out that the biblical statement "And the Word was made flesh" is backwards.[4] We all begin our lives as beings of flesh who are "infants," a word whose Latin derivation means "unspeaking." Words come later as our baby flesh grows and meets the world. The Word is synonymous with a male Creator in the biblical tradition; therefore, putting it before flesh denies that human life begins with women, in the context of a woman's body. "Returning Words to Flesh" is thus an effort to correct the male imagination which has too often passed for gospel truth.

Second, "Resurrecting the Body" cannot be accomplished by traditional religious thought, which originally framed it as the highest achievement of theism. The time-honored masculine desire for transcendence has severely handicapped much of philosophy and theology. Because too many men have imagined themselves as independent of the physical and social circumstances in which they live, the philosophical and religious traditions men have created can now offer little help in addressing pressing environmental and social problems. In order to think more clearly, contemporary theorists need to see the web of physical and social conditions which construct their lives and ideas. Since Western religious thought cannot reveal the physical and social contingency of human life, we must turn to other ways of thinking, such as psychoanalysis and feminism, to resurrect the body.

ONE

Apocalypse in Everyday Life: The Cultural Context in Which We Do Theory

There is a well-known nursery story in which the prophets of the coming disaster call attention to the wrong thing. You probably remember the plot. It all begins when something strikes Henny Penny on the head while she is feeding in her barnyard. She decides that the sky is falling and that she must rush off to tell the king. On the way to do this, she meets three friends in succession—Turkey Lurkey, Ducky Lucky, and Chicken Licken—who are each easily convinced that the sky is indeed falling down. The three fowls eagerly join Henny Penny on her mission to inform the king. They soon come upon Foxy Loxy, who pretends to share their concern and also joins the march. On the way, the fox gobbles up each one of the birds and then falls into a contented sleep. At the end of the fable, there is no one left to tell the king that the sky is falling.

Clearly, the threat that the fowls in the story feel is not imagined. However, they make the mistake of displacing this realistic fear onto something too extraordinary—the collapse of the sky—when it is actually a danger far more immediate and mundane that is about to wipe them out. Further, Henny Penny's belief that high-level help will be useful brings about the tragedy. Her faith in a far-off paternal authority blunts her instinct for survival, makes her blind to what is really happening, and finally, does her in.

Henny Penny is, I suggest, a typical middle-class chicken in a postmodern barnyard. Her sense that the forces of danger as well as those of salvation are operating at a distance from her is a common pattern of contemporary sensibility. Many of us feel her particular anxiety about an apocalypse to come. We are in continual discussion about rumors of a falling sky.

But one difference between those who once spread alarm in the fable and those who are now warning of disaster is that the present prophets of doom are very likely to be right. By making an analogy to the fate of Henny Penny, I am not implying that fears of large-scale future tragedies such as nuclear war are unfounded. The birds in the fable were wrong about their falling sky. Unfortunately, people such as Helen Caldicott and Jonathan Schell are absolutely accurate about their assessment of the danger under which we all stand.

I am using the story of the birds to illustrate a habit of sensibility. There is, I think, a tendency to use the possibility of a future, all-encompassing end to the planet to represent concern about catastrophe within the daily fabric of life. As a symbol, future global devastation focuses our relatively dim awareness of very present, very local threats to vitality— threats which might become central characteristics of Western middle-class culture. I think that just like the fowls in the nursery story, we are disappearing to each other every day; we don't notice that we are nearly gone. We have channeled our anxiety too narrowly and explained it too specifically. The only terrors we allow ourselves to recognize are the huge ones.

Although there are several theorists whose work about modern malaise has influenced me, when I search for ways to explain my feelings about the constriction happening in everyday life, for better or worse, I am drawn to images from films and television. For example, science fiction movies portray modern life as being quite dreadful.[1] Since the 1950s, these second- and third-rate disaster movies have depicted this malaise in an exaggerated comic style. A common formula for these movies is one which shows ordinary people doing ordinary things before the destruction comes and they are forced to cope with terrifying circumstances. Movies about severe earthquakes, floods, and fires, or about rampaging monsters who wreak havoc on a complacent city fall into this category.

The early films were often made in Japan and used absurd monsters like Godzilla and Rodin to represent the holocausts of Hiroshima and Nagasaki. Thus this whole bizarre genre of disaster movie has its roots in the horror of two real apocalypses of recent history. The awkward, primitive film machinery that built the early cinematic monsters paralleled the bumbling technology that constructed the first atomic weapons. As the special effects of our horror movies have become more sophisticated, so have our nuclear armaments.

This connection of the evolution of disaster movies with the development of machines designed to destroy human life can be pushed further. I think the cinematic creatures of the 1950s can be seen as early caricatures of fears about the way daily life was being influenced by more ordinary technology. In the films, it is either the monster or the totality of the devastation which is the most original part of the lives of the stereotyped human characters. There is a sense in which they are already dead before the catastrophe occurs. The huge, horrible thing which arrives is an expression of the death-within-life that I see as a central theme of such films.

The extraordinary monster's relation to ordinary life is depicted quite precisely in my favorite late-fifties horror movie, *The Blob*. In one scene, the Blob, a slow-moving, amorphous dark mass which grows by consuming everything in its path, invades a movie theater. While the audience sits with all eyes transfixed on the screen ahead, the creature enters from the back and begins to roll over row after row of spectators. I see the Blob in this scene as an exaggerated image of the audience's fear of being obliterated by its own increasing preoccupation with the artificial life presented on two-dimensional surfaces.

Scenes in which users of television, movies, or other machines are annihilated in the act of watching or sometimes just listening continue to appear from time to time in the current spectrum of popular entertainment. For instance, in a movie called *Bells,* people are turned into fleshy masses oozing blood while they hold telephone receivers to their ears. However, despite such notable exceptions, contemporary media imagery about technology is generally favorable. There are many films and television programs in which machines, robots, and creatures from outer space are shown as making ideal friends and even lovers. Often these artificial forms of life are shown as having more wisdom, depth, and passion than any human in the story. On the level of their manifest content, these productions seem to be comforting us with the idea that the fears we used to have about machines were groundless and that fake humans are, in fact, better, nicer, and even sexier than real ones.

The television pap which depicts this preference for relationships with mechanisms reflects the general direction of North American culture very well. We are, I think, engaged in a process of making one another disappear by living more and more of our lives apart from other humans, in the company of machines. Occasions for both sustained and casual relations with one another are decreasing, and spheres of activity which once required extensive social interaction are now possible with only minimal human participation. Consider these examples:

1. In play, television and video games make other humans inessential for entertainment and relaxation. Comfort, diversion, and friendly competition can be easily and reliably furnished by a machine. Television talk shows substitute for actual chat, and "buddy shows" about camaraderie replace the real thing. As Barbara Ehrenreich once wrote in *Mother Jones,* the only activity that is never shown extensively on television is the thing that viewers are really doing—namely, watching television for hours on end.

2. In work, colleagues and co-workers are becoming less a part of working life as more people work in isolation at home, on computer terminals, or on other types of machines. Since the factory or office is for many people a last bastion of regular contact with their peers, increasing substitution of the home for the place of work could make alliances such as unions and office romances obsolete. There are now suggestions afoot to broadcast union meetings on television in order to encourage greater "participation." This will probably only create more apathy among workers.

3. In sex, real women and men are less necessary for arousal now that pornography and sexual devices are so widely available. Sex can become a more and more private affair, often involving only one person and the technics needed to inspire his or her masturbation.

4. In reproduction, both women and men can become less important to one another as reproductive technology becomes

more sophisticated. Fertilization does not even require a casual acquaintance between the bearers of the sperm and the egg. Eventually, fetal development may not require a relationship between mother and child.

5. In education, professors are becoming less necessary for students as video classes become more popular. Students also have less contact with one another since they can follow lectures in front of individual television screens.

6. In medicine, many things doctors used to do are now done by machines which diagnose and treat diseases. The physician is often replaced by cold steel.

7. In police work, instead of patrolling neighborhoods, police officers spend an increasing amount of time in cars waiting for radio dispatches. Security work in general requires observing surveillance machines more than it does observing people.

8. In warfare, troops are less necessary for generals now that so much killing can be done automatically.

These are a few examples of how we are making our communal ties to one another less obvious and less physical. I think Marshall McLuhan was right about technology's ability to turn the world into a global village. However, he failed to take sufficient notice of the discarnate quality of the majority of the village's citizens. As we become increasingly more aware of the presence and activities of people all over the globe, we become increasingly less acquainted with the felt physical presence of people in our immediate environment. It becomes very easy for us to avoid each other. We are pushed to prefer the company of machines.

By blurring our sense of the body politic, machines alter our relationship to our own bodies. We use machines for the purpose of extending all our senses and capacities. With machines, we live more, see more, hear more, taste more, play more, work more, travel more, and heal more. Some machines are likenesses of body parts. All are mechanized bodily functions which have been severed from their broader human context in order to expand sensual range and possibility. Machines are supposed to heighten sensibilities and extend life, and in many ways they do. But, paradoxically, the machines which enable us to live more also allow us to feel less. This deadness comes from the progressive dissolution of the social, physical context for human emotions—from the dissolution of our human bodies.

That the physical and social landscape of our culture affects our sense perceptions is one of Susan Sontag's themes in her book *On Photography*. In this series of essays, Sontag explores how the camera has changed our sense of self and world. She writes that there are many ways in which the photographic image has become more real than what we actually see. The camera, she argues, has altered our sense of sight and perhaps has even begun to define reality for us. We often try to see things as cameras do and thus distance ourselves from being involved in what we see. Real seeing becomes dispassionate, "objective," mechanized seeing.[2]

Sontag's work shows how the technology of photography enables us to take the world out of context. Photography allows us to break things up into abstracted images which then seem more real than the things themselves. In fact, reality is often felt to be inferior to its photographic images, with which we are continually bombarded. Women in particular, I think, have suffered from photographic objectification. We have been pictured and posed in order to be formed by the artificial images of ourselves posing. As French feminist Hélène Cixous suggests, culture directed by men behaves toward women as does a photographer-dictator who says, "Hold still, we're going to do your portrait, so that you can begin looking like it right away."[3]

But this is only an example. The point I want to make is more general than the objectification of women by photographic technology. I think both women and men are being pushed to objectify all of life, that is, we are pushed to abstract life like a photographic image and experience it in dissociated parts. It is possible to see a connection between the prevalence of photography in our world and the way many of us feel about that world a good deal of the time.

Machine-age mobility allows relationships and communities to become fragmented and discontinuous. Jobs and career paths lead us away from each other—from our pasts, our friends, our families. Our social groupings are mainly determined by the dictates of the increasingly anonymous institutions for which we work. We live out our lives in a series of places, in a series of relationships. Sustaining a network of friends becomes a Herculean task. Age groups are segregated. Babies stay in one place. Yuppies in another. Old people in yet another. Isolation. The lack of sustained human contact. Transience. The lack of a sense of inheritance. We are all somewhat displaced. We are all very much in mourning. To find comfort, many are drawn into the retreats of private cocoons in front of flickering screens.

I have just painted a bleak picture—too bleak to be completely accurate. What I have not mentioned is that most of us have our own ways of resisting the dominant, lonely, North American technological culture I am describing. Although I think we are all pushed to constrict our range of experience, to dull our sensibilities, and to distance ourselves from one another, I also know that most of us do things to fend off this pressure. We make efforts both to nourish our individual sources of vitality and to preserve our essential human ties. I consider these private modes of resistance to be countercultural, and I hope that we all become increasingly successful at cultivating our own gardens. But I do not think many people can have lasting success at living something different unless resistance to dehumanizing forces takes more public forms.

Perhaps the increased standardization of institutional experience and the concomitant longing for real people in our lives might inspire us to do things differently. Our collective discontent might grow strong enough to create myriad countercultural opportunities—opportunities to understand each other as complex, integrated persons who are in profound relationship to each other and who actually do weave the fabric of each other's lives. I think that those of us who do theory in the humanities have a role to play in creating these opportunities within the "discourses" of scholarship. I think we should be resisting the disappearance of people in the world by working on theory that is countercultural—that is, by working on theory that reveals human presence instead of obscuring it. This will be very hard to do.

One reason I think countercultural theory is so hard to build is that there is actually a great deal of pressure to "celebrate" images of ourselves as mechanisms. I find a disturbing example of such celebration in Sherry Turkle's book *The Second Self: Computers and the Human Spirit*. In the very first paragraph of the acknowledgments, Turkle reveals how the concept of what is "human" has been displaced for her. "I have worked on this book for six years," she writes, "and I have accumulated many debts. My first, of course, is to my informants who generously allowed me to share in their lives. My second debt is not to individuals but to an institution. This is the Massachusetts Institute of Technology."[4] By thanking

15

MIT as if the institution were a live person, Turkle sets the tone for her book. I think Turkle's book demonstrates how hard it is for even very talented humanists to maintain a vision of a nonmechanistic human being while surrounded by people who really do understand themselves in machinelike terms. Her work is a fascinating, sympathetic account of the thinking and aspirations of people at MIT who build their lives around relationships with computers. Throughout her book, Turkle is generally uncritical of the statements of informants who explain that the only difference between themselves and their computers is that they are carbon-based while the machines are silicon-based. At the end of the work, Turkle implies that questions about whether computers are generally good or generally bad are naive. After all, she writes, "no one asks whether relationships with people are good or bad in general."[5]

I do see Turkle's point that we should think much more specifically about the particular social contexts in which particular computers are used instead of making sweeping statements about their goodness or badness. However, I think her equation of relationships with computers to relationships with people attests to the same conflation of human and machine that the people she interviewed display. Her unresisting participation in the world view of the informants results in an all too typical and sanguine vision of our culture—a culture whose future she sees as bringing us "new forms of intimacy with machines, and a new model of mind as machine."[6]

Turkle is wrong when she stresses the newness of the model of mind as machine. This way of thinking about human beings is actually very old. Indeed, the weighty traditions behind the model of human as inhuman constitute another reason why theories that reveal human presence are relatively rare in Western thought. Most forms of Western philosophy and religion have taught that we are inferior imitations of things that are inhuman. I suspect that our centuries-old systems of belief, which have taught us that human life is a rough copy of something out there—something better, wiser, and purer—have laid the groundwork for the modern collective acceptance of machines as models for human selves.

Although the thinking that Turkle describes may well be old, she is right in calling attention to the newness of our increasing intimacy with machines. I suggest that it is this very intimacy which makes the old ways of thinking particularly pernicious. At other times of history, when people lived lives which required more social contact, notions about transcendent entities directing human life were perhaps rather harmless. Perhaps such ways of thinking even provided some inspiration to explore what was behind the facades of material and social reality. But now, because our lives have become so socially dissociated, ideas such as Platonic forms and a God-out-there carry a different valence. They lead us further out of this world and support our tendencies to turn away from each other. Any notion of a superior, absent, bodiless power who is all-seeing yet unseen can only support the stupefying idealization of that which is not alive. Any contemporary form of monotheism can only lend approval to the standardization and homogenization of human experience. These time-honored beliefs of our Western religions—beliefs which are present in varying amounts in Christianity, Judaism, and Islam—are based on fantasies both of independence from matter and of complete domination of the planet.[7] Unfortunately, the human behaviors inspired by these ideas of transcendence and monotheism are coming all too close to creating the nothingness of heaven everywhere on earth. The theories that will

17

prove salvific in this time of our lives as a species are those that oppose our withdrawal from the living—theories that reveal life in its particular, complex, and contradictory forms.

In 1967, in a book called *Reflections on the Nude,* British art critic Adrian Stokes suggested a purpose for art in our world—a purpose which I think can be applied to contemporary theory as well. Art, writes Stokes, should give spectators cause to feel more at home in the surrounding environment just as the artist would have cause to become more at home as a result of doing the work. To do this, art ought to be "bent upon constructing an image for sanity".[8] A sane image, he thinks, always functions in some way to suggest an integrated yet complex human body.

Stokes explains that although viewing the nude is a central metaphor for his argument, he understands that the sense of being at home in the world is fostered by much more than being surrounded with pictures of complete human bodies. The experience of oneself as a continuous, complex being is brought out by contact with more abstract forms as well. Integrated being, he believes, is shown by textures which imply depth and history, by intricacies of patterns in which shapes and lines have relationships, and by architecture in which there is either reference to living form or a cohesion that makes sense to human perception. Observing the natural forms of flowers, trees, and other plants, or watching domestic animals who, he writes, "live out their lives as complicated bodies from nose to tail," are ways many of us have of personalizing "the hive to which we belong."[9]

Stokes is careful to say that art is only one means that we have for providing ourselves with a sense of cohesion in the environment. In fact, he thinks that the disappearance of art as we know it would not matter at all if everyone would become like an artist in work, in interests, and in view of the world. Greater engagement with visions of sanity would count for more than would the styles such engagement might take.

Stokes's idea that the psychological value of art lies in its power to strengthen our sense of ourselves as cohesive beings is derived from the theories of Melanie Klein. According to Kleinian psychoanalytic theory, we begin the lifelong project of sensing relationship among parts of our bodies, our sensations, our emotions, and our thoughts in infancy when we realize that the body of our mother is a whole entity. This perception of the mother as a connected being who continues to exist even though she is at times absent and even though there are times when we hate her is the crucial stage in the development of our ability to feel that we ourselves are complex, whole beings. In Kleinian thought, this issue of our own integration is never completely finished. We are continually in need of having images of wholeness and cohesion fed back to us in order to counter what the Kleinians understand as a universal tendency to "go to pieces."

In *Reflections on the Nude,* Stokes draws attention to the ways in which many contemporary physical and social settings are working to undermine each individual's sense both of being integrated personally and of being linked to the larger world. "I find it disturbing," he writes,

> that we have constructed an urban environment the character of whose undertones does not feed back to us the plain symbols of sanity; the configuration of whose objects has no emphasis for the observer upon their wholeness. . . . What chance have we in cities today to reconstruct the whole mother from her voice? Here in London in the Burlington Arcade one can attend to people who stand and converse amid leisurely sounds

19

of other people walking. A variety of echoes come back from the walls. It seems to me a measure of our plight that such an experience is a luxury to be treasured; apparently a haven from unending explosions of traffic that uncover no space, no amenable distance.[10]

In an atmosphere characterized by auditory, visual, and spatial fragmentation, he thinks that art and other aesthetic experiences should present us with occasions "to feel, in the recesses of the mind, that all human functions are parts of a single and varied entity."[11] However, he continues, because the dilemma is such a pervasive one, solutions cannot be thought of solely in aesthetic terms. Whole societies have to be pushed in various ways toward what he calls "a sober conception of the integrated being."[12]

I think we who do theory in middle-class urban environments can participate in such a project. Like artists, we can try to develop a sense of personal cohesion through the ideas about which we speak and write. Each theory (a word derived from a Greek verb meaning "to see") is actually a particular vision which can influence personal and collective sensibility. Our theories can thus help us to see each other, and even to talk together for extended periods of time.

When Stokes wrote his *Reflections on the Nude* some twenty years ago, he felt that the prospects for what he called "whole objects" were not good. I think the increasing substitution of machines for people has made the denial and distortion of human form and presence even more pervasive now than when the essay was written. Many of the constructs of this culture seem to be just like the mirrored gold-plated buildings which are now so common in our cities. These buildings deny their own mass, interiority, and complexity as you look at them. When you catch a glimpse of yourself in the facade of such a

20

structure, you appear as a shiny, distorted image in a single tint. While the presence of a few such buildings and a few such mirrors is harmless and might even be fun, the possibilities of your experience will be limited if these structures are all you can see or all you can inhabit.

If there is any truth to this analysis of our collective problem, our work as theorists, as visionaries, should be involved with revealing living presence within the ideas, visions, and theories we use. I like the statement Tom Robbins makes at the end of *Still Life with Woodpecker:* "I'll never write another novel on an electric typewriter again," he promises. "I'd rather use a sharp stick and a little pile of dog shit."[13] Such an approach to cultural production would be one way of maintaining a sense of perspective on living form. Any writing produced in the way Robbins describes would have to be read in the immediate terrain in which the work was done. And the physical setting of the manuscript's production would be evident to all. Perhaps all theorists should consider Robbins's vow before composing a single line.

I find some other useful directions in the nursery story with which I began all this. We should remember, I think, that the chickens in the story had a real problem with fragmentation. Although they worried about the future catastrophe of a falling sky, the immediate threat of going to pieces came from the hungry fox who was already right there. They might not have met their doom had they only kept looking at one another. Instead of lining up to tell a distant monarch about what was happening, they would have been better off sitting in a circle and cultivating a very local awareness. They should have forgotten about the king.

So, I think, should we. Preoccupation with idealized far-off authorities can do us no good now. We should be talking

21

theory while never taking our eyes off one another. This might be harder for us than it would have been for the fowls of the fable since we have so many more ways of running off to tell the king and, unlike the animals in the barnyard, we don't see each other every day. Because we hardly ever talk to one another in a sustained way, we will have difficulty in building theory that can do more than reflect the fragmentation of our lives. Under these conditions, waiting for near-perfect theory which can offer nourishing, thoroughly practical visions of ourselves as varied, complex, embodied beings would be as frustrating as waiting for the next messiah.

However, if we do not expect too much too soon, I think we can recognize many efforts in contemporary theory to fight the disappearance of people. In psychoanalysis, for example, object relations theory (in the British and American varieties) is continuing to supplant drive theory. Seeing human beings as constituted by social relations rather than by internal mechanisms reflects a longing for human presence which, I think, has been increasing in Western imaginations since at least the end of World War II. In other fields, such as philosophy and theology, theories of self-in-relation rather than of autonomous selves are, I think, similarly expressive of the desire to conjure up the presence of people in a lonely world. *These theories are motivated by a sense of loss of human contact.* I find great promise in them. I am very attracted by them. However, I feel that unless patterns of social interaction change, these theories will function chiefly as wishes. We will be explaining to ourselves how we really are in relation to each other without living that relation out in meaningful ways.[14]

It is important to remember that the theories of both psychoanalysis and feminism originate in human talk. Both the analytic hour and the consciousness-raising session are forms

22

of conversation. By looking to such social encounters for their inspiration, psychoanalysts and feminists rediscover what Plato and Socrates seemed to have known long ago—namely, that attentive, sustained conversations are excellent sources for the development of theory. Perhaps ideas and techniques within feminism and psychoanalysis still have potential for supporting the radical practice of frequent long talks.

Another current in the West which opposes the disappearance of people is the interest in the traditions of aboriginal peoples or, indeed, in the traditions of any people who live on the periphery of the institutions of global modernity. Although the stirrings of new respect for people who have been victimized by Western hubris, imperialism, and expansionism cannot undo the injustices of the past, perhaps a recognition of the bankruptcy of feeling in the modern West will help restrain future destruction.[15] I consider the interest in cultures which are less lonely than ours to be another sign of the yearning for sustained human presence. Such study might lead to experiments with more satisfying forms of collectivity in this culture.

There are also theorists who are looking to what has been repressed within Western culture to find more vital bases for their visions. Feminist work on networks of female friendship, on lesbian history, on women's religious practices, and on what actually occurs in relationships between mothers and children are expressions of research that operates in a countercultural fashion to reveal patterns of feeling and living that are at variance with the dominant male standards. The interest of theorists in the experience of oppressed ethnic groups also provides resources for imagining alternatives.

In addition, we must pay close attention to work which takes apart the traditional patterns and texts of authority in

Western culture. Deconstruction, whether it is found in literary theory, linguistics, psychoanalysis, history, or feminism, is a seemingly negative force (often much too pretentious) but it nonetheless holds out some hope for teaching us how to look at each other.[16] By searching for the human circumstances, the political ambitions, the erotic longings behind the "great" thinkers and their thoughts, deconstruction, at its best, allows us to see the paradoxical, contradictory human presence which our contemporary culture obscures. Deconstruction is often resisted because it undermines what are imagined to be secure foundations of civilized theory while offering nothing firm to take their place. Yet I think we need such irreverence the way we need air. We need to be continually reminded of the human lives and human limits behind all the theories that have ever been thought. Continuing to mystify the mainstream traditions of Western philosophy and religion by pretending that they reveal essential, God-given, or universal truths, will not enable these traditions to offer us the human ties we need. We must see these theories as man-made in order to assess them properly and to give us practice in looking at one another. Henny Penny was right; the sky *is* falling. We ought to be asking one another what to do about it.

24

PART ONE

Readings in Body Language (Mostly Male)

Reviewing a Mentor: The Concept of Body in the Work of Norman O. Brown

Norman O. Brown was the first major lecturer I heard when I was at college. That was in the mid-sixties when Brown was touring campuses giving talks based on the text of *Love's Body,* a sequel to his immensely popular *Life against Death: The Psychoanalytical Meaning of History.* I was thoroughly impressed with both lecture and lecturer. The hall was packed with an adoring audience who hung on every word of Brown's nervous, intense performance. As I listened to him blend poetry with prose and English with Latin, I remember thinking that hearing him speak was akin to looking through a kaleidoscope. Brown's words cascaded into one another—continually suggesting new patterns and possibilities for both imagination and theory. On that evening, college was an exciting place to be.

I know that it was my memory of that magic lecture long ago that kept me among the handful of my colleagues who did not walk out when Norman O. Brown delivered a plenary address at the 1983 national meeting of the American Academy of Religion. Brown gave a long, dull, seemingly pointless lecture about Muslim military history. He recounted those parts of the Islamic past which relate to fanaticism and bloody battles. I guessed that his exhaustive (and exhausting) treatment of this subject was another expression of his fascination with the idea of violent apocalypse—an interest which sometimes raises its head in Brown's earlier texts. I left that lecture determined to take another look at Brown's work, to try to understand what it was about his thought that had once moved me and many others so deeply.

There is good reason to look back at the task Brown set for himself in the sixties. At that time, he felt that the hope of civilization was "the resurrection of the body." In *Life against Death* and *Love's Body,* Brown tries to build a philosophy of immanence—to chart ways to make discourse and institutions more attentive to the sensuality and physicality of human beings. This project of Brown's is more crucial now because our collective capacity to destroy everything immanent in self and world has become several times greater than it was twenty years ago. The body of the world needs everyone's close attention.

One way of advancing Brown's work is to assess it: to try to understand where he went right and where he went wrong, or to be more precise, to see both how he stayed with what he called "the body" and how he retreated from it. It is my hope that such an assessment will highlight the strengths of feminist theorists who are now writing about psychoanalysis and also writing their own philosophies of immanence.

Brown's focus on the human body was inspired by Freud. "The aim of psychoanalysis . . ." Brown writes, "is to return our souls to our bodies, to return ourselves to ourselves, and thus to overcome the human state of self-alienation."[1] Brown succeeded in persuading many readers that psychoanalysis had a message and a mission that deserved their attention. "The step," writes Susan Sontag, which Brown takes, which moves beyond Freud's own conception of what he was doing, is to show that psychological categories are also bodily categories. For Brown, psychoanalysis (and he does not mean the institutions of current-day psychoanalysis) promises nothing less than the healing of the split between the mind and body. . . . We are nothing but body; all values are bodily values, says Brown. The core of human neurosis is man's incapacity to live in the body—to live (that is, to be sexual) and to die. Psychoanalysis is conceived by Brown not as a mode of treatment to smooth away the neurotic edges of discontent, but as a project for the transformation of human culture, and as a new and higher level in human consciousness as a whole.[2]

Brown maintains that the chief resource of psychoanalysis in the task of cultural transformation is its uncompromising insistence on the primacy of the human body. To him the body was complex—a historical variable involving emotion, memory, and politics. For Brown the psychoanalytic push to uncover physical motives behind every thought, image, ideal, and enterprise is salvific for our civilization. He reverses the common criticism that psychoanalysis is a "reductive" mode of thought leading nowhere. This so-called reductionism, he argues, is the only hope for a sane future.

Brown repudiates Jungianism and much of neo-Freudianism for refusing to stay with the body. He writes that "the fundamental orientation of Jung . . . is flight from the problem of the body, flight from the concept of repression."[3] According to Brown, when theorists of any stripe abandon the psychoanalytic "command to relate the human spirit (and its creations) to the human body," they abandon physicality "and then inevitably have to return to autonomous spiritual concepts and norms traditional in Western culture and challenged

29

by Freud."[4] For Brown, losing sight of the body means giving up all hope for a "scientific criticism of society."[5]

Life against Death suggests that repression in human history could end through the triumph of a science based on what Brown calls the "erotic sense of reality."[6] This goal could be realized, he believes, if psychoanalysis becomes effective social criticism. Freudian theory could reverse humanity's tendency to substitute "the desexualized or deadened life" for "the reality of living-and-dying."[7] Such a reshaped psychoanalysis could then revitalize culture.

But Brown calls for more than a psychoanalytic critique of culture. He wants psychoanalysis to become central to economics, science, and religion. Because these institutions of modern culture disregard the facts of human carnality, he finds them naive about how fantasies arising from human bodily experience influence their own theories.

For Brown, contemporary economics is the study of how to condense and store money, which, he argues with characteristic overstatement and flair, is "filthy lucre" or excrement. Thus the manipulation of money has its roots in a human fondness for playing with shit; and shit, according to Brown, is the quintessence of dead matter.[8] Brown quotes Ruskin to voice the hope that the study of economics, instead of continuing its preoccupation with the accumulation of lifeless money, could teach "nations to desire and labor for the things that lead to life."[9]

Brown's formulation of a psychoanalytic critique of science centers on the "morbid" tendency in scientific thought to operate solely from the "partial impulses" of possessive mastery over nature. He asks, "What would a non-morbid science look like?" His answer is that "its means would not be economizing

30

but erotic exuberance. . . . It would be based on the whole body and not just a part; that is to say, it would be based on the polymorphous perverse body."[10] Brown deplores the guise of objectivity cloaking modern science. He wants the involvement of scientists in their projects to be made apparent. With this challenge, he anticipates recent feminist theories which construct a more elaborate critique of science and its claims to objectivity.[11]

It is Brown's writing on religion that is probably his most quoted work on the theme of how fantasy based in the body constructs ideology. In a brilliant, irreverent chapter on Protestantism, Brown insists that the key to Luther's reform of Christianity is the fact that Luther was defecating when he realized the truth of God's justice. In Luther's privy theology, the devil functions as the lord of shit—which is equated with the entire material world. Thus basic to Protestantism is a view of the world as nothing but excrement, dead matter that can only be redeemed by God's transcendent splendor. Although he praises Luther for expressing repressed anal feelings in his theology, Brown regrets the "massive withdrawal of Eros . . . from life in this world" which Protestantism encourages.[12] Brown looks to psychoanalysis to counter the Christian tendency to loathe the flesh. He feels that any wish "to rise above the body is to equate the body with dead excrement."[13]

It is close to this point in *Life against Death* that Brown contradicts his entire argument. He envisions life freed from the deadening repression of the body as thoroughly idealized and completely disembodied. The passage is striking in its dissonance with the logic of the rest of his book and thus warrants careful attention:

31

If we can imagine an unrepressed man—a man strong enough to live and therefore strong enough to die, and therefore what no man has ever been, an individual—such a man having overcome guilt and anxiety, could have no money complex. But at the same time such a man would have a body freed from all the sexual organizations—a body freed from unconscious oral, anal, and genital fantasies of return to the maternal womb. Such a man would be rid of the nightmares which Freud showed to be haunting civilization; but freedom from those fantasies would also mean freedom from that disorder in the human body which Freud pitilessly exposed. In such a man would be fulfilled on earth the mystic hope of Christianity, the resurrection of the body, in a form, as Luther said, free from death and filth. Freedom from filth would be freedom from the infantile fantasies which concentrate libido on the excremental function. . . . Freedom from death would be freedom from that dominion of death-in-life which Luther grasped as the dominion of Satan; but the freedom from death would be the strength to live-and-die. "What has become perfect, all that is ripe—wants to die."

With such a transfigured body the human soul can be reconciled, and the human ego become once more what it was designed to be in the first place, a body-ego and the surface of a body, sensing that communication between body and body which is life.[14]

Brown's retreat from his own insight seems incredible. How could he imagine that a life lived in the body would be free from "disorder" and "infantile fantasies," free from "death and filth," free from the "sexual organizations"? After thinking so astutely about the flight from physicality, how could he idealize his "unrepressed man" as an air-brushed Mr. Clean who exists in a calm steady state free from genital wishes and bad dreams? "These few lines," writes Ernest Becker commenting on the same passage, "contain fallacies so obvious that one is shocked that a thinker of Brown's power could even let them linger in his mind, much less put them down as reasoned arguments."[15]

This bit of text about a type of Superman reveals the ambivalence that Brown feels about life in the body. He cannot accept human physicality as vulnerable and alive with desire, but instead continues to participate in what he terms the "Christian hope" for a "transfigured" body, a perfect body beyond the pettiness and triviality of actual flesh. The deathlike quality of Brown's wish for perfection is apparent in his idea that his "unrepressed man" would be "ripe" and thus quite willing to die. In truth, if the unrepressed man were to live the passionless, static life that Brown describes, there would be no need for him to be willing to die. He would, in fact, be already dead.

The body which Brown depicts in *Life against Death* is impossible to particularize, impossible to touch. What would the "unrepressed man" do from day to day? In order to be free from the "disorder of the body," this man could never be hungry, ill, or even tired—could never feel vulnerable, or even ambivalent. Such an abstract description fits neither old men, who certainly experience the limitations of their bodies, nor male infants, who are subject to the intense physical needs and sorrows of babyhood. The unrepressed man could thus be neither young nor old. Nor could he be female, for how could one who is free from the disorder of the body ever menstruate, give birth, or go through menopause?

Dorothy Dinnerstein finds it impossible to imagine Brown's ideal human involved in the chores of motherhood. I agree. Indeed, how could anyone be free from thoughts of what Brown calls filth and still be involved in the burping and diapering of babies? "In *Life against Death*," writes Dinner-stein, "one senses mothers and their offspring still somehow tucked away together in nurseries while men roam about enjoying the polymorphous eroticism that is their birthright." [16]

Even if we exclude female experience from the range of possible activities for Brown's Superman, we are still at a loss to conjure up any appropriate unrepressed pastime. Moneymaking, that usually respectable male activity, is out, since Brown says that the ideal man would have no money complex. And lovemaking would itself prove very difficult because the perfect being would be free from all "sexual organizations." In fact, *Life against Death* gives the impression that all civilized activities are unsatisfactory sublimations. Because Brown insists on perfect unrepression, he ends up finding every human action imperfect. Although he wants to propose some method of loving the world, he becomes involved in negating it.

According to Becker, Brown's failure to make proposals that can be taken seriously is to be expected. Becker believes that all calls for salvation within "natural existence in the frustrating limitations of the body" are bound to resolve tension through a vision of total transcendence. [17] For Becker, humanity is obliged to continually strive in anguish to get beyond the body. There is not much to be expected from what he calls an "eschatology of immanence" such as Brown proposes. [18]

Becker's criticism of Brown's Christian vision of the ideal, resurrected body is important because it points to a general failing in utopian hopes for the body. Unless theorists are willing to accept the imperfections of human physicality, they will not be able to avoid postulating an apocalyptic solution to the tensions of bodily life. Christianity proposes death as the answer to life through its vision of the perfect, yet dead, resurrected Christ, and Brown winds up doing the same with his deathlike portrait of the completely unrepressed man. To avoid such a negation of life, a philosophy of immanence must be tolerant of ambivalence, complexity, and limitation.

In *Life against Death,* it is important to understand that Brown is, in fact, talking about the resurrection of only one type of body: a male body, and a particular male body at that. He always speaks of an idealized male body that has the social permission to imagine itself as distant from both its own disorder and from the disorder involved in attending seriously to anyone else's body. Brown focuses on this particular male body, which he calls "perfect," but which he says "wants to die."

This same desire for a perfect male body is, perhaps, the motive behind Brown's frequent criticism of psychoanalysis for having no utopia.[19] Psychoanalysis, he laments, "does not take seriously . . . the possibility of human perfectibility."[20] But in *Life against Death,* his effort to give psychoanalysis a utopian vision—to give it an eschatology imbued with Christian hopes for human flawlessness and transcendence—only offers death. Perhaps one way to get further than Brown does with the "resurrection of the body" is to stay with a more authentic psychoanalytic pessimism about the perfectability of human life.

Instead of resurrecting the perfect, above-it-all male body, which is, after all, the dead, "touch-me-not-for-I-am-newly-risen body" of the New Testament, I suggest that there are better bodies to resurrect. By better, I mean better in the sense that Brown says he means it. One goal of his work is to forge a path different from the one taken by so many Western intellectuals—the path which, he writes, follows "Plato and Descartes over the abyss into the insane delusion that the true nature of man lies in disembodied mental activity."[21] On

35

Brown's terms then, a better body to resurrect—that is, a body in which to ground our thinking and dreaming—is a collective body, which I suggest is for nearly everyone remembered as a maternal body. Thinking based on a maternal body cannot support deadly notions of autonomous, perfected transcendence. A maternal body is always, I think, a relational body, experienced as a matrix alive in herself and yet, at the same time, serving as a physical and communal context for other human living.

The maternal body I am talking about is alive in both male and female memories of the physical connection and dependency of infancy and childhood. Thus this body-as-matrix is an experience that both men and women know but that women have been required to know better. Because adult women continue to live out of a body politic in their roles as mothers, caretakers, and supporters of the activities of men and children, women in general seem to be more conscious of the social matrix of which they partake, and which, in turn, partakes of them. In contrast, because adult men are permitted to imagine that they are no longer the bodies in matrix they once were as children, they tend to believe, speak, act, and write as if they were autonomous bodies. In fact, men, like women, always exist as matrices. As adults, they are bodies embedded in a plural, contradictory, ever-changing body politic. Like all mothers, they have an active part in creating this collective body. The extreme dependence we all experience in infancy and childhood is an essential condition of human existence—a condition that should permit men both to remember and to consciously live out what I am calling the "maternal body." The body-as-matrix is a political experience potentially available to men if the social world would only demand it of them.

36

After *Life against Death* was published, Brown began to express an increasing awareness of the social nature of all thought and discourse. The form and content of his next book, *Love's Body*, elaborates a vision of body that is more maternal. Instead of using a unitary structure for his chapters and an expository style, he writes *Love's Body* in fragments, as a pastiche of quotations and commentaries on quotations. He designed his pages, he says, to include "the references in the body of the text" as a "perpetual acknowledgement of my indebtedness to a very great company, both living and dead" who authored the book with him.[22] In a later book, *Closing Time,* he quotes James Joyce to make the point that writing is always embedded in a social body: "Really, it is not I who am writing this crazy book. It is you, and you, and you, and that man over there, and that girl at the next table."[23]

We should learn, writes Brown, to see printed words as lace on the page, "to see between the lines . . . black on white; or white on black, as in the sky at night, or in the space on which our dreams are traced."[24] The fragmented quality of Brown's text reveals that each written sentence rests on much that is not written, that each conscious thought is the visible portion of processes invisible and often unconscious. The spaces between the passages acknowledge that the reader is also present in the writing—that the reader is there to fill in the blanks.

This breakdown (or meltdown) in Brown's text is, I think, a result of his conscious effort to let go of the idealized monarchic mode of thought and performance which he criticizes as "phallic." Early on in the book, he writes about going beyond Freud to Melanie Klein in order to recognize the influence of the mother's body on the formation of symbols, thought, and institutions. Throughout *Love's Body,* he sprinkles quotations from British object relations theorists such as Joan Riviere and Ella Sharpe, who stress the importance of the social environment in the development of individual and collective sensibilities. "We are members one of another," writes Riviere.[25]

To reveal the live, collective body in which we all take part, Brown thinks our language should be rich in image and symbol. He understands metaphor to mean metamorphosis. Speech that uses symbols is transformative because symbols demonstrate linkages. Every symbol says that one thing is like another and thus testifies to an unconscious conviction that all things are interrelated. For Brown, speech alive with imagery could lead to a broader sense of participation in human and nonhuman environments. He reflects sporadically on the illusory boundary between "body" and "world." "The body . . . is identical with environment," he writes.[26] Metaphor, for him, functions to express the unreality of our separation from nature.

Furthermore, according to Brown, metaphors show "a subterranean passage between mind and body."[27] Every word begins from a sense of particular physical being and reaches outward: "No word is metaphysical without its first being physical."[28] But in order to promote the connection between what is felt to be mind and what is felt to be body, he thinks that language must be allowed to evoke many meanings, to be polyvalent and polymorphous. Words must be allowed to flow into one another in order to become new things and to foster an erotic sense of reality. Brown appreciates the psychoanalytic method of free association. Speech, he thinks, must be free to make associations, to form attachments.

The longing for connection, he realizes, is impossible without a sense of loss. It is the recognition of a void in things which motivates creation and exploration. "Freedom in the use of symbolism," he says, "comes from the capacity to experience loss."[29] Words should point to a void, should reveal their own transparency in order to encourage a sense of nothing at the heart of things. "Admit the void," he urges, "accept loss forever. . . . Wisdom is mourning; blessed are they that mourn."[30]

It is this sense of loss which Brown is unable to maintain in *Love's Body*. The poignancy of desire and imperfection within human life leads him to yearn for apocalypse. Consider, for example, a passage from his chapter titled "Fire."

> The true body is the body burnt up, the spiritual body. The unity is not organic-natural unity, but the unity of fire. "But first the notion that man has a body distinct from his soul is to be expunged; this I shall do by printing in the infernal method, by corrosives, which in Hell are salutary and medicinal, melting apparent surfaces away, and displaying the infinite which was hid." The apocalyptic fire burns up the reality of the material world. In the baptism of water we are buried with Christ; in the baptism of fire we are conformed to the body of his glory.[31]

With this text, Brown again expresses his desire for a transfigured body—that is, for a dead body. He wants the physical body burnt up, changed, and made "spiritual." Violent transformation is his answer to the tension of living within the limits of a human body. Once again, he seizes the image of Christ's resurrected body as his idealized vision of escape from that tension. The specter of a body punished for its imperfections and purified by fire haunts the last chapters of Brown's book. I think it was this fascination with violent purification which in 1983 moved him to recount the gruesome details of the Islamic holy wars.

The task of bodily resurrection that Brown began in the 1960s is today being carried forward by feminist philosophers and theologians. Feminist theorists can now take the "resurrection of the body" much further because they are not enamored, as was Brown, with praising a mystified male version of embodiment. Examples of viable feminist philosophies of immanence abound.

For instance, we see writing that resurrects the body in *The Newly-Born Woman,* a text by Hélène Cixous and Catherine Clément.[32] Cixous sees the hysterics of the past as the culture-creators of today. She says that we women had to express our dreams and visions literally in our bodily symptoms. Now we can write out those visions and bring that turbulent energy into the bodies of our texts. Sexualized experience becomes textualized.

Like Brown, feminist theorists experiment with forms that are more fluid, multivocal, and thus reminiscent of what I call the maternal body. Cixous and Clément avoid publishing a pat monovocal book by ending *The Newly-Born Woman* with the script of one of their arguments. Freer forms are also sometimes used by theorists such as Julia Kristeva and Luce Irigaray. These writers, though very different from one another, share a concern with letting a variety of moods and feelings animate their work. An example is Kristeva's essay titled "Stabat Mater"—a text in which she describes lying down with her infant son and recalling her own infancy.[33] Mother/child and grandmother are thus present in the work. Almost any of Irigaray's writings, with their rambling and partial sentences turning back on one another, suggest the "plurality" of style and "the mechanics of fluids" which are often her subjects.[34]

I also see a maternal body being resurrected in the themes chosen by feminists in theology and religious studies.[35] The late Nelle Morton focused on the idea of being "heard" into speech. Thus Morton brought the social, maternal background of theory to the foreground. She reminded us all that no woman speaks very well unless she is confident that someone is listening.[36]

Elisabeth Schüssler-Fiorenza's work shows that religious ideas, like literature, arise out of very specific political/social matrices. Schüssler-Fiorenza analyzes the New Testament texts to reveal them as complex human products which are sometimes liberatory and sometimes oppressive. By illuminating the social conditions which have given rise to oppressive formulations, Schüssler-Fiorenza loosens the grip of dogma. She breaks up the fetishized text and changes it, we can say, from stone into bread—to use the terms of her own maternal, nourishing metaphor.[37]

Further, the maternal body is invoked by those writers inspired by Goddess symbolism. Carol Christ, Christine Downing, Starhawk, and others show how reflection on female imagery gives rise to different theologies, thealogies, or as Downing once said, to different "thea-erotics." Those interested in Goddess religions are in various ways concerned with articulating the psychological, environmental, or ritual matrix that grounds religious thinking about both gods and goddesses.[38]

Feminist theorists are expanding our understanding about how we create discourse and theory out of our physical, social bodies. In this sense, their work continues the project begun by Norman O. Brown in the 1960s. His work was an attempt to return words to flesh, that is, to show how embodied life is expressed in language. I think his writing should be considered a harbinger of thinking we can now see flourishing all around us.

THREE

On Hockey Sticks and Hopscotch Patsies: Reflections on the Sexuality of Sport

The essay that follows was the first bit of writing I did on the theme of physicality and culture. I had begun my own analysis some two years before and was starting to see the whole world from a psychoanalytic perspective, that is, from a perspective that views all human culture and behavior as alive with emotional, somatic meaning. I began to understand that even the most straightforward physical acts such as breathing and eating were resonant with memories, pleasures, and longings that differ with the particular history of each human life.

My growing interest in the symbolic dimensions of physical actions led me to think about sports. I realized that the highly stylized patterns of human movements that characterize our games and sports must be full of meaning in the psychoanalytic sense. Since the elaborate rules of the games we play are neither random nor arbitrary, they must be expressive of complex human motives, both conscious and unconscious. My work on the sexuality of sport is an effort to see what some of those motives might be.

The essay is true in the way a joke is true—that is, it exaggerates one aspect of a human situation to create an effect.

When I wrote the essay, the male domination of public culture seemed very funny to me. I wanted to capture that playful mood on paper. The two essays that flank this work on sports, one about the male, Christian body within the texts of Norman O. Brown, the other about the tribal imperative to have an identity, are heavier explorations into masculine hegemony. I have placed "On Hockey Sticks and Hopscotch Patsies" between these two weightier pieces to provide a bit of comic relief.

One winter evening, my friend Eta and I were ordered to "get the hell away" from the snooker table at Canada's National Press Club in Ottawa. My husband, Bob, who had brought us there as his guests, was reprimanded as well. "Get them out of here," an old journalist shouted. Bob defended our right to be there and we, with our sticks in our hands, stayed where we were.

Later, the man who had been so rude apologized—he had had too much to drink, he had had a fight with his wife, etc., etc. A few weeks after that, I read about the difficulties female snooker champions had with being allowed to play in important tournaments. Even though one of them had sunk "144 balls in a row," men were still finding ways to keep her out of competition. Most professional snooker players clearly considered it a man's game. I had been thinking the same thing myself.

Snooker, like pool, is played with sticks which are used to shoot balls into holes. The best snooker players are those who have the greatest control of their sticks and balls. They are those who can "call their shots," who can predict which ball they will shoot into which hole on a given shot. In the bars and billiard halls of the world, men take pleasure in competing with one another over the issue of who can best control his stick and sink the largest number of balls into a particular hole.

Snooker is not the only game in which men compete with one another over their ability to use sticks to control balls. Because I live in Canada, hockey leaps to my mind as well. A hockey puck is a somewhat flattened version of a ball. The use of sticks in hockey is far more elaborate than in snooker. The sticks are not only used to shoot the puck into the hole (which in hockey is a framed opening made into a saclike structure by means of a net), but are also employed to interfere with other players' efforts to control the puck. Players use their sticks for varying sorts of offensive and defensive purposes. A defenseman's chief function is to jealously protect his goal from approach by any member of the alien team. The goalie in hockey is permitted to use his whole body as well as his stick to prevent a foreign player from implanting the puck within the home goal sac.

As in the case of snooker, female hockey players have been strongly discouraged from playing on male teams. While it is true that not many women have shown much inclination to play hockey with men, whenever a young female player does, she is booted out of serious competition early. A few years ago, officials ruled that females simply could not play in tournament games of the Junior Hockey League competition. A nine-year-old girl who was an ace hockey player was disqualified from playing with her team when this decision was made. Like the snooker table, the hockey field remains largely an all-male preserve.

In Canada, hockey dominates the world of sports. Millions of men are devoted both to playing the game and to keeping track of the doings of myriad teams. They watch the game on television, listen to it on the radio, read about it in the print media, and discuss it endlessly among themselves. Little boys as young as five and six are outfitted with costly equipment and trained in the skills the game requires.

This male passion for hockey causes vast amounts of money and effort to be expended. Star hockey players are heroes who receive enormous salaries. Cities construct arenas for the sport. Newspapers and magazines employ specialized staff to photograph the games and write about them in great detail. Radio broadcasters build careers on their ability to convey the excitement of hockey action. Television stations routinely postpone the late news in order to show viewers every minute of the hockey events being covered each week during the season, and most nights during the playoffs.

This expenditure of money, energy, and resources on the propagation of male stick sports is one reason why women ought to pay attention to the games. In addition, because such sports seem to play a central role in the way men talk (and possibly think) about what they do on their "teams" in other arenas such as business and government, women need to see the games clearly in order to comprehend male culture beyond the playing field. We need feminist theory about sports because the exclusion of women from male groups occupied with using sticks to chase balls into holes parallels the exclusion of women from male groups doing more serious stuff elsewhere in culture.

We can begin our efforts at a deeper comprehension of the games men play by noting that, for the most part, it is men who are fascinated by both playing and watching the stick variety of team sports. I hasten to qualify this statement. I am well aware that women can and do play very fine hockey, lacrosse, polo, golf, etc. I am also aware that, to a certain degree, these sports are of interest to both sexes. Men and women enjoy using their bodies in ways that demand strength, agility, and endurance. In addition, both sexes appreciate watching members of either sex use their bodies in ways that challenge muscle and mind. However, I maintain that it is chiefly men who are drawn both to watch stick sports and to participate in them. Female players and female fans are less attracted to the dramatic configurations of the games than they are to the opportunity to observe human physical prowess. It is the male imagination that thought up stick games. We women watch the sports and sometimes even play them because very often "it's the only game in town."

I suggest that all stick sports involve players and audience in intense phallic drama. Male sexual desire is portrayed as a force to be channeled by elaborate sets of rules. The symbolism and organization of the games seem to depict an adolescent male's struggle to focus his sexual activities into the channels and goals his culture condones. Perhaps the holes and goals of the various stick games represent the vaginas of the women with whom mating is permissible. If so, then placing the permissible goal in the foreign team's territory might be an expression of an incest taboo urging the male players to try for intercourse (to "score") outside their own family or tribe. Such a deeply rooted incest prohibition might be operating in the rules of several types of stick sports and would explain why players are never allowed to shoot at the goals of their own teams. Only exogamous unions of ball and goal are permitted. Only they will be cheered by the crowd.

An incest taboo might also explain why, in snooker, the white cueball is forbidden to enter any of the pockets on the table. In this game, because any player may (theoretically at least) try for any pocket on any shot, the location of the goal sacs indicates nothing about endogamy or exogamy. All holes are open to all balls of all colors. Without restrictions on the white ball, perversion and promiscuity would run rampant on the table. In such a situation, the white ball can stand for propriety and social order only if it remains completely chaste—aloof from immersion in any hole.

In addition to dramatizing the cultural fact that only certain orifices are considered to be appropriate spaces for male incursion, the phallic theater of stick sports also depicts male concerns about competition among penises regarding issues of strength and agility. A young player learns that he must control the movement of his stick in order to aim it accurately. He must shoot well to direct his seminal fluid—that is, the ball or puck—into designated locations. Missed shots are like premature ejaculations and, because semen never enters the goal cavity, everyone feels a bit disappointed. (Good sportscasters capture the collective sense of let down in their commentaries.)

I believe that the hypothesis I am framing here—namely, that phallic fantasies are at the root of stick sports—is equally valid for foot sports such as soccer, rugby, and football as well as for hand sports such as basketball.[1] I rely on an important psychoanalytic principle to support the transposition of symbolism from sticks to hands or feet: Freud notes that it is common for phallic symbolism to be "displaced" upwards or downwards from the genitals onto other body parts. In Freud's explanation of *Oedipus Rex,* for example, Oedipus puts out his own eyes as a gesture symbolizing self-castration.[2] Further, the name *Oedipus,* which in Greek means "swollen foot," can itself be understood as alluding to the improper sexual act in which the unfortunate man's penis becomes involved. Thus this classic drama about one man's wayward genitals illustrates both upward and downward displacement of phallic imagery.

47

I think similar displacement is at work in sports in which the penis is symbolized by feet, hands, or even heads.

Although the phallus is imaged somewhat differently in the symbolism of foot and hand sports, I believe that the ball continues to symbolize seminal fluid just as it does in stick sports. Nevertheless, there are times in football, rugby, soccer, and basketball in which the ball also seems to represent a penis—a penis only to be touched by particular players in particular ways at particular times. In contrast, in the stick sports, the perpetually stiff piece of equipment which symbolizes the penis can usually be held continuously throughout the game.

In all male team sports, contact with the ball is subject to elaborate controls. If, as in basketball, hands are permitted to touch the ball rather freely, then kicking is absolutely forbidden. Or, as in soccer, if feet are allowed frequent contact with the ball, then many restrictions are placed on manual manipulation. These rules probably reflect cultural restrictions on touching the penis or on having erections in inappropriate places at inappropriate times. I have heard several men discuss the embarrassments they suffered as adolescents when they were unsuccessful at controlling the erections of their rambunctious organs. Some also felt much remorse at succumbing to urges to masturbate. No wonder that the games men and boys learn when they are young dramatize their desire for mastery over the phallus! The fact that some forms of ball games (most notably rugby) have been cultivated in all-male British public schools supports this view of the games as exercises for teaching genital discipline.

The phallic drama enacted in such stick games as baseball and cricket is somewhat different from the games I have discussed so far. In baseball, for example, each team member

48

takes a turn at attempting to hit the ball instead of having to compete for the opportunity of making contact with it. The issues involving the bat seem to be the clear male genital concerns of all stick sports: how hard can the bat hit the ball; how far can the ball be made to go; how accurately can the hard-hitting bat direct the ball into areas that meet with social approval. The main focus of baseball would thus seem to be on the strength of the phallus of each individual player. A similar contest is acted out in carnivals when men swing mallets to see how far up a stick they can drive a ball. If the ball goes to the top ("all the way"), a bell rings.

In baseball, however, another issue comes into play besides that of pure phallic power. This additional concern relates to the contamination carried by the ball once a player has hit it. The ball/semen of the player must not actually touch that player once he has made contact with it. If the player is tagged with the ball he has hit, he is considered polluted and declared "out." Indeed, the ball must not even symbolically touch the player by arriving at a base before he does. As long as the ball is directed away from the player after his hit, he is safe and can cavort around the bases. But the fun is over as soon as the ball comes back to his body. Perhaps the avoidance of the ball in baseball is an expression of social prohibitions against masturbation that forbid men to be preoccupied with touching their own semen. Or perhaps the message is closer to one that I have already noted in stick games, that is, that sexual liaisons must be sought outside the home area with partners outside the tribe. Probably the symbolism is multilayered and refers in a general way to taboos against both masturbation and incest.

One conclusion that could be drawn from this type of reflection about men's games is that all sports which take place either on a field (hockey, soccer, etc.) or on a table (pool, snooker) spring from phallic fantasies. In 1923, Melanie Klein drew just such a conclusion:

> In the cases of pleasure in motion—games and athletic activities—we could recognize the influence of the sexual symbolic meaning of the playing-field, the road, etc. (symbolizing the mother), while walking, running and athletic movement of all kinds stood for penetrating into the mother. At the same time, the feet, the hands and the body, which carry out these activities and in consequence of early identification are equated with the penis, served to attract to themselves some of the phantasies which really had to do with the penis and the situations of gratification associated with that organ.[3]

Although I understand why, given the prominence of phallic symbolism in Western games, Klein would reduce all bodily motion in sports to an identity with the phallus, I do think we must not be so quick to see phallic action as all there is (or all there could be) in organized play. For example, there are other things going on in net games such as tennis, badminton, volleyball, and ping-pong. These types of play might be expressive of a less specific sexuality than that displayed in the forms of sport I have looked at so far.

Although net and court games often make use of paddles and rackets, I think these implements are not quite equivalent to the phallic sticks of hockey and snooker. Although paddles and rackets certainly express some phallic symbolism, for the most part they function as simple extensions of the hand by broadening the range of palms and fingers. I am more willing to consider games such as tennis, badminton, and volleyball as less focused on the phallus because these games are often

50

played in circumstances that are not segregated by gender. (Think, for example, how men and women can be mixed on both sides of the net in volleyball—a game which is often organized when people come together for informal sporting exchange.) The fact that women and men frequently play net games together indicates to me that these sports emphasize something other than phallic competition among men in which women can only be symbolized by goal-sacs, posts, or pockets.

In net games, a ball or "birdie" is moved at a varying tempo across a net between the territories of two people or two teams. The analogy with sexual intercourse comes to mind. Perhaps the net is the body boundary between two people and the ball is a generalized symbol for the fluids and feelings which pass between people during sexual activity. Net games seem to be more concerned with the give and take of sexual relations between equals.

In some games of exchange such as handball, racquetball, and squash, the net has become a line which divides two players who stand next to one another instead of face to face. Such games are possibly expressive of homoerotic desires. Since these court games are most often played by pairs of men or women, the side-by-side arrangement might well be placing emphasis on the fundamental sexual sameness of the players. Of course, by speculating on the homoerotic quality of court games as opposed to net games, I am not implying that enthusiasts for any given game are predominantly either heterosexual or homosexual in their more literal sexual practices. A homoerotic sporting preference would probably prove compatible with a generally heterosexual lifestyle and vice versa. Since we are all bisexual beings to differing degrees, it is quite

51

natural for our civilized sporting life to express a spectrum of sexual feelings. Sports should be an arena in which a range of physical and fantasy experience can be enjoyed.

So far, I have proposed three sporting categories:

1. Adolescent male games which emphasize phallic competition among men: hockey, soccer, rugby, football, polo, basketball, baseball, cricket, golf, snooker, and pool.
2. Adult games which emphasize sexual exchange between the sexes: tennis, volleyball, badminton, and ping-pong.
3. Adult games which emphasize sexual exchange between members of the same sex: squash, handball, and racquetball.

These categories leave out something very important the clitoris. If this theory about sexuality in sports has any validity, there have to be games that are built around the specifically female imagery of the clitoris. Examples of such games can be found. Consider a famous fairy tale about a young princess and her golden ball. I quote the beginning of Tom Robbins's version of the story in his novel *Still Life with Woodpecker:*

> Once upon a time, a long time ago, when it was still of some use to wish for the thing one wanted, there lived a king whose daughters all were beautiful, but the youngest was so lovely that the sun itself, who had seen so much and forgotten so little, simply marveled each time it shone on her face.
>
> This daughter had a favorite plaything, a golden ball, that she loved dearly. When the days were hot, she would go out into the dark forest near the palace and spend many an hour tossing and catching her golden ball in the shade of a leafy tree. There was a spring in the forest, and usually the princess played near the brink of the spring so that when her play made her thirsty she might take a cool drink.
>
> Now it happened one day that the golden ball, instead of falling back into the maiden's little hands, dropped to the

52

ground and bounced into the spring. The princess followed the ball with her eyes as it sank, but the spring was very deep, and it soon sank out of sight. The bottom of the spring could not be seen. Thereupon she began to cry, and she wailed louder and louder as if her little heart were broken.[4]

The princess does retrieve her golden ball. Almost immediately after the accident, a frog appears and promises to return the toy if the princess will let him be her companion—if she will let him eat with her, drink with her, and sleep with her. She promises and the creature fishes out the ball and returns it to her. However, the princess soon finds the frog too disgusting to have around and tries to break her promise. When the king insists that she keep her royal word, the desperate princess hurls the frog against a wall in a violent attempt to free herself from his repulsive presence. As soon as he hits the wall, the frog becomes a prince who marries the now-ecstatic princess. The two live happily ever after, and we never hear another word about the golden ball.

Robbins speculates about the toy's disappearance: "Maybe the princess put aside the golden ball until her own children were old enough to play with it, or maybe once she had a prince to play with she simply abandoned her beloved toy. . . and it got packed away in an attic, thrown out with the garbage, stolen by a chambermaid, or donated to Goodwill Industries."[5] In any case, after the princess meets the prince, the ball no longer claims her attention. "Whatever happened to the golden ball?" remains an often-posed but never answered question for the characters in Robbins's novel.

According to the classic Freudian interpretation Robbins mentions, the frog in the story is really a penis, which, although initially repulsive to the young girl, soon becomes alluring to the young woman. Although Robbins does not explain the ball in psychoanalytic terms, it seems obvious that it is the clitoris—which according to a Freudian tale has to give way to the vagina as the seat of sexual pleasure in order for a girl to develop a "proper" sexual response. Seen in this way, the story reads as a piece of patriarchal propaganda expressing a male wish for women to give up all pleasure in their own bodies and learn to take sole delight in the penis. From the prince's point of view, the princess's ball is to be forgotten. Presumably if she were to maintain her interest in her toy, she would be less involved with what her prince has to offer. I take it as a sign of Robbins's identification with his women characters that he is very curious to know "whatever happened to the golden ball?"

I know where we should look for the ball. I think it lives on in the play of little girls who, year after year, generation after generation, bounce it around against walls and on sidewalks. It lives on in the games of jacks and hopscotch in which girls are fascinated with patterns of tossing and retrieving small rubber balls or roundish toys called "patsies." Most of these little ball games involve either hopping and jumping around a patsy (as in hopscotch) or tossing a ball under a leg and bouncing it against a wall or sidewalk. Often rhymes are recited to emphasize the rhythmic quality of such play. Having the ball between the legs seems crucial to these games. Even jacks, which involves hands and fingers more than it does legs, is a game which often takes place between a girl's legs as she sits on the sidewalk, tosses the ball in the air, and picks up the jacks in patterns of onesies, twosies, threesies, etc.

In all little ball games, there are elaborate rules about how and when things can be touched. Bouncing ball games involves rules about what must be done between bouncing the ball and catching it. For example, sometimes a girl must clap three times or turn around twice before she catches the ball she has thrown against the wall. In more complicated games such as jacks, there are more complicated restrictions on touching both the ball and the jacks. A girl playing jacks can only touch the jacks she intends to pick up while the ball is in the air. If, for instance, she touches a third jack while gathering up a pattern of twosies, she loses her turn. She can continue her play only as long as she can manage to touch some jacks and avoid others in the proscribed patterns.

Rules against improper touching are fairly intricate in hopscotch as well. A hopscotch player must throw the patsy within the space of each chalk-drawn numbered box. If the patsy touches a chalk line, the player usually loses her turn. (In some neighborhoods, she is given a second chance to toss the patsy within the chalk box.) Rules about touching also extend to instructions about picking up the patsy once the toss is made. The player must hop through the design of chalk boxes in numerical sequence without ever touching a line with her foot. When she stops to retrieve the patsy, she must use just one hand while she stands on one foot in an adjacent box. If she falters and touches the ground with her other hand, she loses her turn. Thus a good hopscotch player is one who has learned to discipline her body so that she can toss and retrieve the patsy within a small and fairly rigid grid. Could this elaborate use of small spaces be one way little girls train to make maximum use of the restricted social territory in which they will have to move when they grow up? Little ball games warrant study as symbolic expressions both of young girls' psychosexual interests and of the socialization of those interests.

It is striking to note how many little ball games involve throwing and retrieving things. Perhaps this feature of these games shows female interest in an in-and-out movement of

55

things. Or perhaps tossing the ball and bringing it back might express the going and coming of the nourishing breast in particular or of parental attention in general. Indeed, the variety of groupings (onesies, twosies, threesies, etc.) in a game such as jacks could indicate a basic plurality in female erotic interests. The psychoanalytic musings of Luce Irigaray, who theorizes about the complicated dynamics of female sexuality, might illuminate our understanding of little girls' games.[6]

In our culture, the golden ball is neglected, just as it was in the fairy tale. There are no international hopscotch tournaments. Public culture is built around male-run institutions that glorify the hockey puck and scorn the hopscotch patsy. While the games expressive of female sexuality are confined to childhood, the phallic sports of boys are aggrandized to become major cultural obsessions. Girls, for the most part, must watch or play boys' games. As adults, women do not get to flesh out more expansive versions of the games they played as children. We cannot know what little ball games might become if girls were given the physical space and social encouragement to develop sporting patterns that are shaped by their female bodies.

Freud once suggested that limitations on human thought could be traced back to restrictions placed on masturbation. He thought that the way we learn to direct physical energy affects the way we channel mental energy and that our sense of what is physically permissible affects what we allow ourselves to consider as intellectually possible. Perhaps the relative paucity of patterns of sport in our culture reflects both the rigid gender arrangements and the restricted sexual activities we practice.

But all this could change. If our gender arrangements and sexual behaviors were to become less restricted and less stylized in the future, our ways of thinking about ourselves and of organizing our social interactions would change also. And along with the groupings that we have yet to form and the thoughts we have yet to think, there are games we have yet to play. Who knows, one day at the Super Bowl, the princess's golden ball might reappear.

The Tribe and I: Thoughts on Identity from a Jewish Feminist Atheist

The question "Who am I?", can never be asked independently of a social context. Further, the answer we give the question is always selective. What counts as an answer, that is, whether class, race, religion, politics, gender, profession, age, sexual orientation, or mother tongue will be singled out as a crucial factor varies from epoch to epoch, and from country to country. Who I am is always both a matter of who I feel I am and who you let me be. Because we are all continually constructing one another, our identities have some flexibility. This conviction that the social body is mutable makes me somewhat optimistic about our collective human future.

I believe that anyone who can discuss the factors that give her or him an ambiguous sense of identity has something important to teach. Since, in varying degrees, many of us are confused about who we are, we need voices to address that confusion—voices that explain how an identity is not a simple given, but rather is always conditioned by past history and present circumstance.

The conditioned, complex nature of identity is something I have learned from the intersections of my triple perspectives as a Jew, a feminist, and an atheist. I have learned to enjoy playing these parts, which are possibilities for me within my culture. Each identity has something to offer.

I grew up as one of the only Jewish kids in a predominantly Christian neighborhood. I thus encountered a lot of crosses around other children's necks. I always saw these images as stop signs. To me they said, "Go away. This means you. I am a cross around a Christian neck and I am worn to keep children like you at a safe distance." I remember feeling some sympathy for those vampires who were said to be warded off by garlic necklaces as well as by crosses. My schoolmates' assertion of their membership in the Christian club that excluded me made my Jewish identity a bit monstrous, and I grew up feeling hurt and rejected by crosses, crucifixes, and most other Christian paraphernalia. (Christmas trees were an exception. Those wonderful, essentially pagan things never made me feel unwelcome.) That feeling of rejection still lingers. I cannot look at a cross without feeling some sadness and anger. This feeling of exclusion is also present to a smaller degree when anyone wears a cross verbally—that is, when anyone triumphantly declares, "I am a Christian."

As a child, my defense against the rejection posed by crosses could have been to don a Jewish star. I had several in my jewelry box, including my favorite, a star my father had found lying in a German street after the war. But I never felt comfortable wearing a Jewish star. Perhaps I didn't want to be singled out as someone so very different. Being crossless was hard enough.

Even when I went to high school and had a majority of Jews in my class, I still didn't join many of them in wearing a star. Now my sense of difference was the result of economic factors.

The Jews with whom I went to high school were generally the children of well-to-do professionals. My family was more lower class and could not afford the high cost of membership in a local synagogue. So although I was befriended by many of my classmates, I felt the economic inequalities as a vague sense of not belonging to my Jewish peer group.

The result of these early experiences of exclusion causes me, in the opinion of some Jews, to "lack a strong sense of Jewish identity." One friend labels this "tragic" and feels that my ambivalence toward Judaism is a weakness depriving me of a useful standpoint from which to contribute to my culture. I disagree.

The experience of being a relatively poor Jew within a wealthy Jewish community in a predominantly Christian environment makes me an uneasy member of any social group in which I am included. While a part of me relishes the acceptance, another still maintains the perspective of an onlooker, an outsider. When I am at my best, my particular Jewish history makes me sensitive to the ways outsides and insides are constituted. As perennial outsiders, many other Jews have had a similar interest that has led them to develop trenchant social commentary. These are the Jews who merit Isaac Bashevis Singer's description as "people who can't sleep and who don't want anyone else to sleep either." It is the practice of social critique that gives me a Jewish tradition in which I can take part.

In the late sixties, such difficulties with Jewishness helped make me and many other Jewish women receptive to the feminist movement. (It is ironic that the call for feminist reform of Judaism itself began gathering momentum only at the end of the 1980s. Jewish women have been an integral part of the secular women's movement for more than two decades.) I think that Jewish women like me who could never find real community within Jewish groups were attracted to feminism because it offered membership in a community of other critical and self-critical outsiders. At their best, feminists have been continually engaged in understanding how gender intersects with other factors to determine status and privilege. Feminists have shown how differences between male and female genitalia are used as signs to proscribe different lives for men and women—lives which vary greatly from culture to culture and from time to time. The continual feminist reflection on human difference has made it difficult, if not impossible, to speak about any universal, noncontingent masculine or feminine nature. Indeed, the very concept of "essential" biological differences has itself been rendered problematic since no perception of male and female uniqueness can ever be separated from its political and social underpinnings. Thus the feminist movement has enabled many women who feel oppressed by race, class, religion, or nationality to articulate their reflections on oppression and to think more clearly about how human difference translates into social script.

Immersion in feminist thought about difference has shown me that we humans are an essentially heterogeneous species that teems with possibilities of feeling, thinking, action, and inaction. I have come to understand human differences as both monumentally important and always contingent. Our cultures—whether of gender, nationality, class, or religion—now appear to me to differ from one another according to which human possibilities they permit and which they discourage. Under different conditions I would have a sense of self very different from what it is now. I could have been, or indeed could yet become, many different people.

This fluidity within my own identity would not have become apparent to me without exposure to feminist reflection about male patterns of thought.[1] The work of some theorists

61

suggests that conventional ideas about a person's need for a single, unambiguous identity arises from male anxiety about bodily stability. This line of thinking makes some sense to me. Men do seem to be obsessed by the fear that they might lose a part of their bodies. As Freudian theory has long maintained, castration anxiety looms very large in the male psyche, and such a powerful fear must influence men's conception of who they are.

What explains castration anxiety? Culture which demands that men radically cut themselves off from identification with their mothers might engender it. But whatever its complex origin, when men are permitted to build the world according to their worries and wishes, the fear of castration seems to become an important foundation of culture. It can, perhaps, be argued that men defend themselves by maintaining masculine territories in their social groupings. Men in groups are always issuing orders which say: "This land is mine. These women and children are mine. These men take orders from me." Male identity often seems to be built around a concept of the tribe and its territory as anxiously guarded parts of the masculine body. In many cultures, including our own, if man B's group claims whatever A considers his territory and has access to A's women, A feels angry and defensive, as if he were cut off from a part of his own body.

Men's need to aggrandize their bodies is, I think, shown in the custom of giving wives and children the male's surname. A man can never have the same certainty about connection with a baby as can the woman who gave birth to that baby. In order to allay insecurity about both bodily integrity and paternity, men might well construct social orders which impose a clear tribal loyalty on their women and children. Patriarchal social order thus might evolve out of a jealousy which demands that allegiance be pledged to only one husband, one father, one God, one country, and one people.

I have transgressed patriarchal propriety by marrying out of my tribe and by having a child with a man who is not Jewish. Because this deed often makes me an object of censure within Jewish circles, I have a personal interest in understanding why the maintenance of tribal integrity is so important to so many.

Rabbis seem especially prone to accuse women like me of threatening the Jewish people with imminent extinction by giving birth to children of "mixed" parentage. They make this accusation even when, according to Jewish law, a child is considered Jewish when the mother is Jewish. I find it strange that few rabbis seem to realize that their harangues against traitors who intermarry are actually diminishing the Jewish community by driving away the great number of Jews who have found spouses among gentiles.[2]

One prominent Canadian rabbi, W. Gunther Plaut, in a famous lament that typifies rabbinical rage against intermarriage, once explained that children of mixed marriages do not have the correct sense of Jewish "peoplehood" even when these children are raised as Jews and given a proper Jewish education.[3] For a long time, I wondered what this rabbi could possibly mean by such a concept of "peoplehood." Now, finally, with the help of contemporary feminist theory, I think I understand.

I think that what bothers Plaut is that children of mixed marriages tend to have a double sense of identity. Even if a child is brought up as a Jew, the fact that one of her or his parents derives from alien lineage must eventually intrude upon the child's consciousness. Such a child might then feel some sense of kinship with another human group as well as with the Jewish people. The oneness of the child's identity would thus be disrupted and, what the rabbi defines as a proper Jewish sense of "peoplehood" would prove impossible.

Unfortunately, such insistence on allegiance to only one group is not confined to rabbis. Nearly all religions in the world now function as monotheisms ruled by a single male God who is thought of as conferring authority on a select group of male directors. Christ, Mohammed, Moses, Yahweh, Buddha, Confucius, the Reverend Moon, the Church Fathers, the rabbis, the priests, the College of Cardinals are central focal points for millions of lives. Further, secular states, political parties, and multinational corporations maintain the emphasis on male authority by treating their male leaders with a loyalty and reverence that mirrors religious practice. Thus male tribal hierarchy with its insistence on unity of allegiance and the separation of groups largely defines the terms of human association on this planet.

Perhaps things could be otherwise if enough women would stop acting as cheerleaders for their men's tribal affiliations. The female sense of diversity within selfhood could offer some alternatives to the particular male scripts which now organize the world into competitive, warring tribes. Men might well have plural possibilities within their identities which the feminist movement could encourage. Growing concern about the violence which is supported by the tribal system may furnish sufficient impetus for change.

There are feminists who reject the suggestion that the capacity to tolerate diversity might originate in bodily experience that is particularly female.[4] They believe that the feminist call for radical pluralism is the result of women's growing political awareness. If we do not learn to relate to each other across differences, say these feminists, we may soon have no world at all. Thus new ways of organizing the human community must be found—ways that transcend the old system of competitive tribal allegiances thought up by men. Audre Lorde frames the argument this way:

> The future of our earth may depend upon the ability of all women to identify and develop new definitions of power and new patterns of relating across difference. The old definitions have not served us, nor the earth that supports us. . . . We have, built into all of us, old blueprints of expectation and response, old structures of oppression, and these must be altered at the same time as we alter the living conditions which are a result of those structures. For the master's tools will never dismantle the master's house.[5]

As I see it, a grand mission for feminism is to dismantle the master's house and to set about building new houses for both women and men. Feminism should demand a thorough examination of all prejudices, all stereotypes, and all enforced separations of human beings along male tribal lines. Perhaps the idea that we each must feel an intense loyalty to a single tribal entity, such as a ball team, a nation, a race, or a religion, is not only outdated but actually dangerous. Instead of insisting on rigid boundaries for any subgroups of the world's population, we should be encouraging a plurality of identifications. Our entire human civilization is in serious danger unless we can reduce tensions among nations, races, and religions. Being a loyal, docile member of a single tribal group does not offer salvation any longer, if ever it did. Now the world is in need of people who can feel several loyalties, several affinities, several identities. Our best hope for a continued human history might well be the construction of a world community whose members feel themselves to be parts of many different human lives.

Feminism can loosen the grip of old identities. When we identify ourselves as women, we disobey the old patriarchal insistence that we group ourselves according to male tribal patterns. We blur the boundaries of nations, abandon absolute loyalty to the founding fathers, and create some chaos. Survival as a species could depend on this chaos, on the breakdown of paternal/fraternal clans whether those clans are families, countries, corporations, or religions. As a practice, as a discourse, as a revolutionary strategy, feminism can help to transform the human community by questioning the established social groupings and by encouraging us all to realize how much we are implicated in the fate of one another.[6]

Feminism, of course, is not the only social movement with an interest in breaking down national and tribal allegiances. For example, organizations concerned about global food shortages point out how the planting of a crop such as coffee or sugar cane in one part of the world for export to North America often makes local populations dependent on unreliable external food supplies because farmers no longer cultivate products for domestic use. The presence or absence of food in a particular country is therefore often determined by consumer demand in another country. Likewise, environmental groups teach that acid rain, PCB's, and oil spills do not respect national boundaries. The peace movement decries the system of strong national identities because that system fuels the nuclear arms race. Blind loyalty to a single national or ethnic group is thus being challenged on several fronts.

I realize that there is an attractive clarity and comfort in claiming a single identity. Furthermore, for many people, strengthening ties with a particular religious or ethnic group is an effective means of resisting the technological monoculture which is spreading throughout the globe. Nevertheless, I

66

think that developing our collective capacities to feel empathy, involvement, and identity beyond our particular tribes is essential. Defensive retreat into exclusive, xenophobic groups is a practice which cannot provide enduring security.

I think that the breakdown of tribal organization can be helped by a certain degree of atheism in the world. I can become evangelical about atheism. All the religious documents which I have read about the "scourge" of atheism seem to me very misguided. Atheists are, in fact, essential to a better world. Atheism is "peopleism." Since it is people who pose the greatest threat to each other, and since only people can save each other, atheism reflects an important reality. "Now that we can nuke God," says a friend of mine, "we had better think seriously about each other."

The concept of God, I find, diminishes people. It lets us deceive ourselves about what we are doing and encourages us to disguise our human agency. Many concepts of God mystify our tribal patterns with notions that a particular group's behavior derives from God. Thus many concepts of God allow us to disguise our own subjectivity, or the subjectivity of clerical rulers, as "divine will." I think we will be much safer if we insist on understanding how we human beings have made our history, our ideas, and each other than if we pretend that there is some sort of supernatural agency at work outside ourselves.

I can imagine preaching a sermon in which I insist that it is the moral duty of every religious person to live at least part of her or his life as an atheist. I would urge atheism as a program for consciously stepping out of tribal patternings for at least some of the time and for experimenting with nonreligious forms of community-building. Perhaps some of the good things that have chiefly been available within religious traditions can flourish elsewhere. For example, the inspiration and

67

sustenance to be found in some mystical practices could perhaps be fostered in secular groups.

If commitment to secular groups is not possible for theists who have derived much of their nourishment from their sense of religious identity, then I would suggest that these theists live part of their lives as polytheists. A polytheist would be obliged to acquaint herself or himself and her or his children with more than one religious perspective in order to encourage the capacity for empathy with people seen as "others."

Although atheism is, in a sense, my calling, I do feel that having a religious affiliation might not in itself be a harmful thing. Perhaps there need be nothing wrong with being a Christian or a Jew, a Muslim or a Hindu, as long as these identities are not used as walls against feeling connection with anyone else. Being a member of a religious tradition should not, I think, become a program which sets up rigid priorities of concern for the particular group considered one's own.

In her poem "Siren Song," Margaret Atwood reveals the magic words that lure men to their destruction, to their fragmentation on the rocks. The song is a cry for help. "Help me!" sings the female siren. "Only you, only you can, you are unique."[7] It's a lie, says the siren, but they want to hear it—and they believe it every time.

I think it's time that we women stopped telling men—and stopped telling ourselves—all versions of that particular lie. It's time we stopped puffing up the illusion that unitary tribal identities are important to our salvation. Perhaps those of us, like me, who hold grudges against the tribal system can help in small ways to dismantle it.

PART TWO

Escape from Jung: Psychoanalytic/Feminist Critiques

Archetypal Theory and the Separation of Mind and Body: Reason Enough to Turn to Freud?

I began my work on Jung's thought by critiquing the sexism within his theories.[1] I soon realized, however, that Jung's concept of the feminine is part of a larger problem in his work. It is in Jung's theory of archetypes that I find the flaw which deforms his entire psychological system. I now understand that any way of thinking which posits the existence of transcendent entities that direct human thought and behavior tends to be both anti-woman and anti-life. My criticism of Jung's sexism has thus evolved into not only a serious critique of the central tenets of Jungian theory but also of other religious perspectives that are based on similar notions of disembodied forces. In this essay, I discuss why post-Freudian approaches may offer a viable corrective to such theological systems.

Forms and Archetypes: Immaterial Forces of the World Beyond

The ancestors of the Jungian archetypes, the Platonic forms, were said to be transcendent entities that were reflected in the physical world, but were most definitely not *of* the physical world. The Platonic forms could be known by the soul. In contrast, the body in Platonic thought was a flawed, impermanent thing which did not warrant much attention. "I spend all my time," says Socrates, "going about trying to persuade you, young and old, to make your first and chief concern not for your bodies nor for your possessions, but for the highest welfare of your souls."[2] The twofold task of the philosopher is to know the world of timeless perfection beyond body and all physical reality and then to help others to gain access to this glorious sphere.

Likewise, in Jungian theory, the psychologist's task is to lead others to see the timeless archetypal reality behind their personal psychological experiences. Jung credits Plato with discovering the reality behind what we usually perceive.

> In the products of fantasy the primordial images are made visible, and it is here that the concept of the archetype finds its specific application. I do not claim to have been the first to point out this fact. The honor belongs to Plato. . . . If I have any share in these discoveries, it consists in my having shown that archetypes are not disseminated only by tradition, language, and migration, but that they can rearise spontaneously, at any time, at any place, without any outside influence.
>
> The far-reaching implications of this statement must not be overlooked. For it means that there are present in every psyche forms which are unconscious but nonetheless active—living dispositions, *ideas in the Platonic sense,* that preform and continually influence our thoughts and feelings and actions.[3]

Jungian archetypes, like Platonic forms, influence the physical world but are not of the physical world. They are understood as transcending material reality. Jung stresses this transcendence in his last major statement on archetypes in *On the*

Nature of the Psyche, written in 1954. In this essay, Jung speculates that perhaps "psyche and matter are two different aspects of the same thing."[4] If this is so, he reasons, then archetypes "as such" must be distinct from their representations in symbols and images and must lie beyond psyche. He coins the term "psychoid" to name this locale beyond both body and soul. These "irrepresentable" archetypes, Jung insists, "describe a field which exhibits none of the peculiarities of the physiological."[5] "Their chiefest effect," he explains, lies in "spirit."[6]

Throughout *On the Nature of the Psyche,* which lays down the metaphysics of archetypal theory, Jung continually compares the archetype to more scientific-sounding concepts. He tells us that the archetype is "analogous to the position of physiological instinct" and states that when "psychology assumes the existence of certain irrepresentable psychoid factors, it is doing the same thing in principle as physics does when the physicist constructs an atomic model."[7] The practice of using scientific analogies to explain archetypes is common in Jung's earlier writings as well. Sometimes he associates archetypes with instincts, presenting the "hypothesis that the archetypes are the unconscious images of the instincts themselves . . . that they are patterns of instinctual behavior."[8] At other times, he uses metaphors from chemistry or physics, such as the comparison of an archetype "to an axial system of a crystal, which, as it were, preforms the crystalline structure in the mother liquid."[9] These scientific comparisons are often cited by Jungians concerned with popularizing archetypal theory.

It is important not to be misled by the frequent use of scientific analogies to explain the notion of archetypes. Science proceeds from the assumption that the composition of matter and energy can be known by means of careful observation and precise measurement. Jungian psychology starts from the premise that the physical universe is controlled by unseen, irrepresentable, and ultimately unknowable forces that are transcendent to the world itself. Although Jung sometimes refers to archetypes as within the stuff of matter, he quickly returns to the idea of the "content" of the archetype as something separate from people and physicality; archetypes are thus far removed from the sphere of science.

The idea that our thoughts, our feelings, and our fantasies are largely influenced by entities outside of our bodies and our physical environment is a gross departure from the major premises of psychoanalysis laid down by Freud. In *On the History of the Psychoanalytic Movement* (1914), Freud writes:

> Jung's modification [of psychoanalysis] loosens the connection of the [psychological] phenomena with instinctual life; and further, as its critics have pointed out, it is so obscure, unintelligible and confused as to make it difficult to take up any position upon it. Wherever one lays hold of anything, one must be prepared to hear that one has misunderstood it, and one cannot see how to arrive at a correct understanding of it. . . . The truth is that these [Jungian] people have picked out a few cultural overtones from the symphony of life and once more failed to hear the mighty and primordial melody of the instincts.[10]

As interesting as Freud's remarks about Jung's theories may be, I have not included the quotation to illustrate Freud's contempt for Jungian thought. Freud's comments underline the essential difference between his approach and that of Jung. Freud insists that psychological phenomena are linked to physical, instinctual life. In contrast, Jung seeks to minimize the influence of bodily experience on the formation of human thought. Much Jungian theory would have us believe that the contents of our minds—our ideas, our motivations, and our fantasy images—are controlled by forces completely divorced from flesh, physicality, and social context.

"So what?" I hear my readers asking. "What is so terrible about a theory which sees human life as determined by non-physical forces?" I believe that understanding the consequences of such thinking is crucial to the future development of theory which can enhance life.

The Case against Splitting Mind from Body

Separating the "mind" or "soul" from body is certainly a well-established practice in Western thought in general and in Western religious philosophy in particular. Whichever way the dichotomy is worded, body comes out as the thing less valued, while mind or soul is seen as more permanent, more noble, and closer to the sphere of divinity.

It makes little difference whether the contrast is drawn between body and mind or body and soul. The important point is that one thing—mind or soul—is seen as qualitatively different from physical existence, as *separable* from the physical world and definitely superior to it. Although formulations of the soul/body or mind/body dichotomy can vary widely among philosophers, all will agree that one entity exists in some sense apart from the other, is better or higher than the other, and is meant to prescribe, to rule, or to govern the other. Indeed, there are many ways of naming the higher parts. Plato generally employs the term "forms," Jung uses the word "archetypes." Religions use the word "God" in singular or plural form. In each case, the better thing is seen as more or less disembodied. Although minds, souls, forms, archetypes, and gods are conceived of as interacting with the physical world in various ways and to various degrees, they are all said to be things apart, things that exist independently of this or that merely physical representation. The better thing is always thought to be closer to mind, while the worse thing is seen as nearer to body.

Debate about the mind/body split has proceeded for centuries among philosophers and religious theorists. It is only in the past few decades, however, that the rather abstract discussion about mind and body has taken a pragmatic turn. Thinkers other than professional philosophers and theologians are developing important critiques of mind/body dualism. These critiques insist that thinking in terms of the separateness of mind and body has serious effects—effects that constrict freedom in human life and perhaps pose a threat to all life on the planet. A survey of certain writers who criticize the mind/body split because of the behavior it encourages will, I think, make very clear why contemporary theory, in particular feminist theory, should shrink from all systems which preserve the mind/body dichotomy.

"In 1953," writes Norman O. Brown in his introduction to *Life against Death,*

> I turned to a deep study of Freud, feeling the need to reappraise the nature and destiny of man. Inheriting from the Protestant tradition a conscience which insisted that intellectual work should be directed toward the relief of man's estate, I, like so many of my generation, lived through the superannuation of the political categories which informed liberal thought and action in the 1930's. Those of us who are temperamentally incapable of embracing the politics of sin, cynicism, and despair have been compelled to re-examine the classic assumptions about the nature of politics and about the political character of human nature.[11]

76

From this quotation we can see that Brown's famous reappraisal of "traditional schools of thought" was motivated by a sense that something was deeply wrong with the theories that informed political systems. He and others articulate the idea that civilization suffers from what it represses. According to Brown, the key to understanding this repression lies in the work of Sigmund Freud.

Brown's work extends some of Freud's theories about the death instinct and about infant sexuality. He uses these ideas to construct the hypothesis that civilization's suppression of bodily pleasures is propelling us all in the direction of death. Brown thinks that we are gradually killing ourselves by becoming increasingly detached from our own bodies and increasingly interested in projects and machines which are opposed to life. "The dehumanization of man," he writes, "is his alienation of his own body."[12] Our flight from our bodies is motivated by a flight from death. Paradoxically, this desire for escape pushes us to a flight from life. "This incapacity to die," Brown says,

> ironically but inevitably, throws mankind out of the actuality of living; which for all normal animals is at the same time dying; the result is denial of life (repression). The incapacity to accept death turns the death instinct into its distinctively human and distinctively morbid form. The distraction of human life to the war against death, by the same inevitable irony, results in death's dominion over life.[13]

It was in 1959 that Brown articulated his vision of a society losing touch with its own physicality and thus losing touch with its own potential for life and joy.[14] In the decades since, as both pollutants and nuclear weapons have proliferated, the symptoms of the problem Brown identified have become even more apparent. Other theorists, motivated by the same social conscience which stirred Brown, have been able to be much more specific about the damage wrought by systems of thought and action which despise the body.

The recent work of ecologists and feminists has questioned the separation of mind and body with an urgency new to philosophical discussion. Ecologists suggest that our environment is suffering from the notion that body (in this case, the body of the earth) is not of central importance. Their argument is that the portion of Western philosophical tradition that deprecates physical existence is in part responsible for the physical abuse that we have heaped on our planet and its plants and animals.[15] The age-old separation of mind and body may thus have abetted the inflicting of real damage on the earth.

Feminists point to another kind of damage which is done by separating the mind and body—that is, damage to women. Several feminist writers argue that the oppression of women is linked to the identification of women with bodily nature.[16] It has even been suggested that the equation of women with "mother" nature reveals that the misuse of the environment and the oppression of women have much in common.[17] The existing body of feminist theory is so rich and varied and has raised so many issues around the consequences to women of the mind/body split that it argues powerfully for all future feminist theory to be firmly grounded in an understanding of the body's role in cognition.

Simone de Beauvoir was one of the first to draw the attention of feminists to the injustice of equating only women with body and nature.

> But to say that Woman is Flesh, to say that Flesh is Night and Death, or that it is the splendor of the Cosmos, is to abandon terrestrial truth and soar into an empty sky. For man also is

flesh for woman; and woman is not merely a carnal object; and the flesh is clothed in special significance for each person and in each experience. And likewise it is quite true that woman—like man—is a being rooted in nature; her animality is more manifest; but in her as in him the given traits are taken on through the fact of existence, she belongs also to the human realm. To assimilate her to Nature is simply to act from prejudice.[18]

Woman, argues de Beauvoir, represents body both because her "animality is more manifest" and because her sociopolitical situation leads her "to stress the importance of animal nature." But both sexes, she insists, must recognize and cope with the problematic reality of bodily existence.

As a matter of fact, man, like woman, is flesh, therefore passive, the plaything of his hormones and of the species, the restless prey of his desires. And she, like him, in the midst of carnal fever, is a consenting, a voluntary gift, an activity; they live out in their several fashions the strange ambiguity of existence made body.[19]

De Beauvoir's analysis of women vis-à-vis the mind/body split has been interpreted as a recommendation for women to transcend the body and be more like men. Elizabeth Spelman criticizes de Beauvoir for this in her article "Woman as Body: Ancient and Contemporary Views." "Although de Beauvoir doesn't explicitly say it," Spelman writes,

her directions for women are to find means of leaving the world of immanence and joining the men in the realm of transcendence. Men have said, de Beauvoir reminds us, that to be human is to have mind prevail over body; and no matter what disagreements she has elsewhere with men's perceptions and priorities, de Beauvoir here seems to agree with them. Explicitly de Beauvoir tells us not to be the people men have dreamt us up to be; but implicitly, she tells us to be the people men have dreamt themselves up to be.[20]

I do not share the view that *The Second Sex* suggests that women reject the body and turn to mind. Instead, I read de Beauvoir's work as a nuanced description of women's situation. I agree with Dorothy Dinnerstein that de Beauvoir's "implication is that in the very act of recognizing . . . truth, we will have started to surmount it."[21] Nevertheless, Spelman's criticism of *The Second Sex* raises an important point. What is the solution to the problem of seeing women primarily as body? Surely it does not lie in seeing women as primarily mind. Spelman argues correctly that the anti-body course which some feminist writers have suggested can only lead to a dead end. Instead of trying to ignore our bodies' relationship to cognitive processes, we should be trying to understand that relationship more profoundly. Only then can we achieve a true comprehension of human thought.

In order to begin to accept our physicality, we must search for theories that explain both why we associate corporeality with women and why we flee our bodies in the first place. We must look for the causes behind the equation of woman and body which de Beauvoir describes. Dorothy Dinnerstein attempts to find those causes in her book *The Mermaid and the Minotaur: Sexual Arrangements and Human Malaise.* Dinnerstein urges us to "look hard at what is very hard to look at." This is "the precise feature of childhood whose existence makes the adult situation de Beauvoir describes inevitable, and the consequent necessity for female abdication of unilateral rule over childhood, which she stopped short of facing."[22]

Dinnerstein argues that our sense of the transience of the human body is complicated by our memories of women as the first caretakers of our bodies. "The relation between our sexual arrangements and our unresolved carnal ambivalence," she explains,

> begins with this fact: when the child first discovers the mystical joys and the humiliating constraints of carnality, it makes this discovery in contact with a woman. The mix of feelings toward the body that forms at this early stage, under female auspices, merges with our later acquired knowledge of the body's transience.[23]

It is because women mother, Dinnerstein believes, that we come to equate women with body and mortality. Our hatred of the body is expressed in our hatred of women. In fact, it is the oppression of women that permits us to make women the scapegoats of our fear of aging and mortality. As long as we hate women, we will fail to come to terms with our bodies and with mortality. We will continue "the self-contemptuous human impulse toward worship of dead automatic things and disrespect for what lives."[24]

Dinnerstein's answer to the problem of the human flight from carnality is to end the female monopoly on early childcare. If men would share the task of caring for infants, it would become impossible to see them as creatures beyond the concerns of human flesh. Women would no longer be scapegoats responsible for fleshly failings. Everyone would thus be forced to come to terms with her or his own mortality.

An end to female-dominated childcare is also a solution Nancy Chodorow proposes in *The Reproduction of Mothering*.[25] Chodorow does not explicitly address the problem of identifying women with body, but rather seeks to explain why women become exclusively responsible for mothering. She concludes that women reproduce mothering to regain the physical and emotional intimacy that they enjoyed with their mothers and that they, unlike men, cannot get from heterosexual relationships. Chodorow's work implies that if men also cared for babies, intense physical intimacy would cease to be an experience that both sexes could only achieve with women. Her argument points to the same conclusion as Dinnerstein's—namely, that women will cease to be disproportionately associated with body only when childcare is in the hands of both sexes. Thus Dinnerstein and Chodorow use psychology to present us with a solution to the problem of equating women and body. Future work in psychology and the social sciences will reveal whether their ideas suggest viable directions that can lead to greater acceptance of both women and body.

Grounding our philosophical, psychological, and sociopolitical theory in a firm awareness of physicality will amount to a major change in the orientation of much of Western thought. Adrienne Rich gives us a vision of that change in *Of Woman Born*. Rich calls on feminists to build theories that "touch the unity and resonance of our physicality, our bond with the natural order, the corporeal ground of our intelligence."[26] She urges us to transform "thinking itself" in order to transform contemporary culture, which she says has "split itself off from life, becoming the death-culture of quantification."[27]

Adrienne Rich asks us to learn to "think through the body."[28] I endorse her plea. As feminist theory sets about constructing new systems of thought, let us make sure that those systems are life-enhancing. Let us not cling to disembodied ways of thinking that lead us to disparage women in particular and physical life in general. We need to show how the much-disparaged bodies of both women and men give rise to all so-called higher intellectual activity. We need to inspire thought that supports physical life by understanding in detail how physical life gives birth to thought.

I suggest that feminist theory should radically depart from the Jungian archetype, from the Platonic form, from all systems of thought which posit transcendent, superhuman deities. We should study these outworn theories as history, and not use them as models for new ways of thought. We must seek our inspiration from theories and disciplines which see the body as the nexus of all human experience.

Freudian and Post-Freudian Psychoanalytic Theory: Directions from the Body

Some useful directions for building feminist theories that "think through the body" might well come from a domain that is midway between art and science, that is, from psychoanalysis, specifically Freudian and post-Freudian traditions. Psychoanalysis has inspired an extensive body of thought based on the idea that human beings are essentially physical creatures whose mental and emotional experience is derived wholly from bodily life. Thus analytic theory should be a natural ally in feminist efforts to explore the "corporeal ground of our intelligence." Unfortunately, this is not the case. The sexism in psychoanalytic theory has caused feminists to reject Freudian and post-Freudian thought almost completely.

In urging feminists to take another look at psychoanalysis, I am not urging that sexism be overlooked, forgiven, or minimized in any way. On the contrary, I want to see feminist critiques of psychoanalysis continue. Freud's theory is undeniably sexist in its stress on the glories of both male anatomy and the male role in society. Because psychoanalytic thought has yet to incorporate an analysis of patriarchy, it is rife with male bias and has never had much insight into its own myopic conclusions about the nature and destiny of women. Feminists must keep pointing out the flaws in psychoanalysis until a feminist perspective informs analysis in both theory and practice.

However, although I support feminist criticism of psychoanalysis (and even plan to contribute to it myself), I maintain that there are other things we should also be doing with Freudian and post-Freudian thought. In addition to criticizing it, we should, I think, be using psychoanalytic theory to give us insight into the physical nature of human thought. We should, in short, be using psychoanalysis to "think through the body."

As an initial step toward using analysis for feminist purposes, I want to note briefly two similarities between feminism and analytic theory. First, psychoanalysis and feminism share the topic of sexuality. As Shulamith Firestone notes in *The Dialectic of Sex,* the focus on sexuality means that Freudianism and feminism "are made of the same stuff."[29] Just as feminists debunk respected philosophical, moral, and religious systems in an effort to uncover sexist agendas, Freudians engage in similar sacrilege when they search for the instinctual foundations of great art and culture. Both groups are continually pushing us to think about sexual motives hidden behind the products and behavior of our "higher" civilization.

Second, Freudianism and feminism both stress the theme of childhood. Psychoanalysis is forever emphasizing the formative nature of childhood and the importance of early experience in structuring adult life. Childrearing is thus a central analytic concern. Feminists also cannot help calling attention to children as they try to improve the economic, political, and psychological situation of women, the traditional caretakers of children. Therefore, in different ways, Freudians and feminists force childhood and childcare to be carefully studied and appraised.

There is much more to be said about the common themes of sex and children in psychoanalysis and feminism. I hope future work in this area will address these issues more directly. Now, however, I want to discuss several specific ideas in the corpus of psychoanalytic thought which will illustrate more precisely what I mean by using analysis to "think through the body." I will begin with Freud's work and then turn to extracts from the work of D. W. Winnicott and Melanie Klein.

I was first struck by the degree to which Freud understands physical and mental processes as being continuous when I read the following statement: "The ultimate ground of all intellectual inhibitions and all inhibitions of work seems to be the inhibition of masturbation in childhood."[30] On the surface, this is a rather astonishing statement (which might well stick in one's mind the next time a writer's block strikes). But the idea makes perfect sense if it is understood as part of the analytic view that the free flow of thought depends on the elimination of repressions. If there are significant areas of the imagination that are blocked from ever approaching consciousness, thought and action will be paralyzed. Since psychoanalytic theorists consider early masturbation fantasies as being especially powerful in establishing the patterns of imagination, inhibitions arising in this area are seen as having long-range effects on all of mental life. The statement that masturbation and creative thought are intimately linked is an example of the way in which psychoanalysis recognizes that the contents of our minds are continuous with everything that has happened, is happening, and wants to happen in our bodies.

Freud is often reproached for seeing all psychical phenomena as derived from sex. It would be more accurate to say that Freud sees all psychical phenomena as derived from the body.

In his final formulation of the principles of psychoanalysis, *An Outline of Psychoanalysis,* Freud defines "sexual life" as "the function of obtaining pleasure from zones of the body."[31] He sees genital sexuality as only a part of the entire physical experience of the individual. Further, he understands that genital sexuality derives from earlier physical experiences involving nutrition, excretion, muscular excitation, and sensory activity. Reproaching Freud for his emphasis on sexuality is, in fact, reproaching him for his emphasis on physicality.

For Freud, genital experience is always metaphoric because it echoes the early intense experiences of infancy and early childhood. In fact, for Freud, all experience is metaphoric because all experience echoes feelings and perceptions that were experienced physically in the deep past. I suppose that in this sense Freudian theory is reductive—in the Latin usage of *reducere*—because it does lead us back, back to childhood, back to infancy, back to states of feeling which are structuring our being but which have slipped from conscious memory. I do not agree with those who think that this direction of Freudian theory diminishes human life. Instead, I feel that looking back in this way deepens experience and grounds it realistically in the physical being and personal history of an individual life.

Freudian theory links mind to body with the concept of the instincts. "We assume," Freud writes, "that the forces which drive the mental apparatus into activity are produced in the bodily organs as an expression of the major somatic needs. . . . We give these bodily needs, in so far as they represent an instigation to mental activity, the name of 'Triebe.'"[32] The *Triebe,* or "drives," come to us in James Strachey's English translation of Freud as "instincts." The question of how to translate the term—whether as "drives" or "instincts"—is not really important. But it is important to understand that by

Triebe, Freud identifies the essential determinants of human life as physical forces. Even though Freud sees the instincts as "mythical entities" which are "magnificent in their indefiniteness," he is certain that they express physical needs and longings.[33] He hopes that one day the theory of instincts will be based on a more precise "organic substructure."[34] Freud envisions an improved instinct theory becoming ever more precise about the physical mechanisms behind human thought.

It is worth stressing the degree to which thought is seen as arising from body in Freudian theory. Psychoanalysis views all of our thinking as motivated by instincts. "The whole flux of our mental life," says Freud, "and everything that finds expression in our thoughts are derivations and representatives of the multifarious instincts that are innate in our physical constitutions."[35] "An instinct," he insists, "cannot be represented otherwise than by an idea."[36] Therefore, in Freudian thought, all our notions, all our images, all our fantasies, and all our ideals have their sources in our bodies. Our mental and physical lives are of one piece—just as a plant is continuous with both its foliage and its roots.

Let me digress for a moment to draw a contrast between the Freudian notion of instinct and the Jungian notion of archetype. Such a comparison will, I think, strengthen my argument for the use of Freudian ideas in theories which are grounded in the body. Instead of instincts, Jung identifies archetypes as the essential determinants of human thought and behavior. Just as Freud modifies the instinct theory, Jung tinkers with the idea of archetypes throughout his work. Both men treat their concepts as provisional ideas to be expanded and delineated by their followers. Despite these similarities, however, instincts and archetypes lead subsequent theory in very different directions.

In contrast to Freud's emphasis on the physical nature of instincts, Jung, as we have seen, stresses the spiritual nature of archetypes. Even though he is fond of pointing to the physical manifestations of archetypes in human myth, fantasy, and behavior, Jung maintains that archetypes are transcendent. This insistence on an extraterrestrial, unknowable component to archetypes encourages much vagueness in Jungian thought. Almost any claims can be made about the unknown and unknowable archetypes that nevertheless are said to determine human thought patterns. The vagueness extends to other Jungian terms derived from the notion of archetypes. "Psyche," for example, becomes a mystical entity in the work of archetypal psychologists. It is often spoken of as something separate from human beings, something which actually animates people's lives but is removed from them. For example, James Hillman states that "of these notions, psyche and human, psyche is the more embracing, for there is nothing of man that soul does not contain, affect, influence, or define."[37] Jungian and post-Jungian thought is thus led to put more value on mystical abstractions than on the experiences of real people. It is led to disdain the literal in favor of the imaginal, to favor what it terms psyche over body and even over human.

Freudian theory, however, can never fly far from what is human and real. Although the theory may err in other directions, it is bound by the emphasis on instincts and by its own scientific method to seek accuracy and clarity in what is known, what is observable, and what is embodied. Freud's stress on the physical nature of the instincts sent psychoanalytic thought in a somatic direction. When psychoanalysts try to understand patterns of human imagination and cognition, they are led to find their answers in the human body.

For another example of how the psychoanalytic approach points theory in a physical direction, I turn to an essay by the

British psychoanalyst D. W. Winnicott. The essay, "Mind and Its Relation to the Psyche-Soma," is particularly interesting to me because in it, Winnicott discusses how bodily experience may itself give rise to a feeling of estrangement between mind and body.

In his discussion of the mind/body split, Winnicott presents the clearest definition of psyche I have ever encountered. His concept of the psyche can clarify just what it is we are studying when we study imagery—whether in myth, art, dream, or reverie. Winnicott defines psyche as "the imaginative elaboration of somatic parts, feelings, and functions."[38] This definition captures what I have always felt as valuable about the concept of psyche and illuminates the vague insights about psyche in the works of Jung and some post-Jungians. Note that Winnicott's idea of the psyche includes no notions of transcendent, out-of-body forces influencing human imagination. Instead, he gives us an understanding of the sense of depth conveyed when we use the word "soul" or "psyche." When we say a person has soul, we are referring to someone who feels her or his physical and emotional being very deeply, who is connected to her or his particular physical and emotional fate profoundly and who somehow conveys that connection.

James Hillman explains soul in a more Jungian way by referring to it as "the imaginative possibilities in our natures, the experiencing through reflective speculation, dream, image, and fantasy—that mode which recognizes all realities as primarily symbolic or metaphorical."[39] With Winnicott's insights we can understand the soul perspective which Hillman discusses without mystifying ourselves about the symbolic activity of the soul. We can see that symbols and images are, very simply, bodily feelings perceived pictorially. Although we might call this type of activity "imagination" and might say that it indicates the presence of psyche or soul, we should still see that psyche or soul is grounded in bodily experience. Thus when we study the artistic works of women to discover the female psyche, we are in fact studying imaginative renderings of female bodily experience. Likewise, when we analyze the imaginative works of men, we are looking at male expressions of physical feelings, drives, sentiments, and longings. The great myths of the world resonate throughout the ages because they capture physical visions that are deep and widely shared. By using Winnicott's understanding of psyche, we no longer have to obscure the impact of myth and art by reference to the magical machinations of disembodied forces such as archetypes, gods, or a superhuman psyche.

After defining psyche as "the imaginative elaboration of somatic parts, feelings, and functions," Winnicott uses this definition to discuss the origin of the idea of mind. He does not "think that the mind really exists as an entity," but that it develops differently in each person as a special function of the psyche-soma.[40] For optimum development of the psyche-soma, he thinks, a perfect environment is necessary. At the beginning of an infant's life, this need is absolute. However, in the normal development of an infant, the environment will, of course, fail to be perfect. This is when the mind develops.

Winnicott believes that mental functioning begins as a compensation for environmental failure. Through cognitive understanding and mental control, the infant transforms the imperfect environment into the perfect one. Mind thus has its origins in the attempt to gain control of the environment.

In the healthy individual, the development of mind proceeds gradually. If the environment is not too unreliable, mind will be felt to be not too distinct from body. However, if the infant's environment is unpredictable, or if the care that the child receives is erratic, then mind will develop as a thing in itself which is felt as very much outside the problematic body and the physical environment. The most common way for this distancing to be imaged, Winnicott believes, is the false localization of the mind in the head.

When I read this theory, three ideas came to my mind. First, if Winnicott is right that the localization of the mind in the head is an attempt to dissociate oneself from a problematic psyche-soma, then theories of transcendent entities located outside and above the mind itself may be efforts to take this dissociation even further. Theories of forms and transcendent archetypes might be symptomatic of the tendency to escape from the psyche-soma and to imagine a degree of outside control.

Second, we should look more closely at the early lives of philosophers who have developed theories that are very much one-sided in their emphasis on the powers of mind and entities beyond. Carl Jung, for example, tells us that at night he feared his mother because he felt she became "strange and mysterious."[41] He thus hints that he experienced erratic mothering. If this is true, it may help to explain his lifelong effort to build a philosophical system which diminishes the importance of people by seeing human destiny as shaped by archetypes.

Third, perhaps Winnicott indicates why it is that anti-body philosophies are so often also anti-woman. If he is right that an intense opposition between mind and body develops when the early environment of an infant fails, then it would be most likely that, in deep memory, a woman is held responsible for that failure, since women have been the most important factors in the environments of most babies. Thus, in cases in which the mind develops as an enemy to the early environment, it might be developing as an enemy to women. This

91

phenomenon could be what is expressed in anti-body philosophy, which is also misogynist.[42]

The hypothesis that the mind forms in opposition to the environment could be used to strengthen feminist arguments that women ought not to be the only people responsible for early childcare. If men were to share the care of infants, women would no longer be seen as the only sex that represents body. Nor would women be the only sex that mind would tend to reject.

Winnicott does, I think, give us a useful theory about the context in which mental phenomena might develop and about how that development might be forming and deforming our philosophies. He points out that the separation of mind from body is an experiential matter. Although mind is essentially a bodily experience, we all feel it in some degree as something separate from our bodies. No philosophy can really change the experiential illusion that mind and body are separate. What can change, however, is our adherence to theories that are based on the illusion of mind/body dualism—theories that disparage bodily life and that keep us from understanding the bodily origin of thought.

Another psychoanalytic idea valuable in helping us to understand why we disparage the body is Melanie Klein's theory linking guilt and sexuality. Klein addresses a question that we should all be asking ourselves whenever we discuss guilt and sexuality: Why is it that sexual acts and thoughts are surrounded with so much guilt? Is it simply because conventional religions and mores have taught that sex is a low and guilt-ridden thing? Or is the relationship between sex and guilt more complex? Do the religious restrictions around sex hide something more frightening than forbidden bodily pleasures?

Klein suggests that the guilt and shame around sexuality are cloaks for another emotion—anger—specifically, anger against parents. To arrive at this hypothesis, she applies Freud's idea that guilt stems from a suppression of the aggressive instincts. She thinks that a child's early sexual fantasies about masturbation are connected in varying degrees with sadistic wishes directed toward the parents. The wishes often involve angry attacks on the parents by means of the child's body and bodily functions. Klein concludes that, "it is the sense of guilt arising from destructive impulses directed against its parents which makes masturbation and sexual behavior in general something wicked and forbidden to the child, and that this guilt is therefore due to the child's destructive instincts."[43]

In psychoanalytic theory, as goes the child, so goes the adult. If Klein is right about the relationship between sexual guilt and anger in the child, then the same relationship would apply to adults as well. We should thus seek the deep origin of feelings of shame, guilt, and contempt for bodies in feelings of anger.

If we look at the story of Adam and Eve in the light of Klein's theory, we can see an interesting motif. In the biblical tale, we are told that Adam and Eve first saw their own nakedness and were ashamed after they ate the apple. Why should this tiny snack have made them so anxious to hide their genital organs? And why should the punishment for their action be as enormous as the one the Almighty dishes out?

Perhaps the guilt and subsequent fantasy of severe and eternal punishment might be explained by the *biting* of the apple. A bite is just about the first hostile action a baby can perform. Although the bite may be a small thing, in the mind of an infant, if Klein is right, it may be accompanied by weighty fantasies of destruction. It is as a consequence of such destructive wishes, Klein believes, that children imagine themselves deserving severe punishment. Because these angry wishes are so closely tied to sexual feelings, when the anger is repressed, the sexual feelings are left tinged with guilt and shame. Thus the fig leaves of the primal couple could have been designed to cover up anger at parental behavior.

Although this interpretation of the apple story may strike some readers as far-fetched, I urge them not to dismiss Klein's insight as quickly as they might this application of it. Anger and its connection with sex is a topic that warrants much attention. We are beginning to see how closely sex and violence are linked in the imaginations and actions of the multitudes who enjoy pornography.

Perhaps the linking of sex and anger is also what lies in the imagination of the multitudes of philosophers and theologians who have written about sexuality with great distaste. It is, perhaps, not sex per se that is shunned, but rather the troublesome angry feelings connected with sex. Klein might very well be right about rage as the key motive behind the disparagement of sexuality in Western philosophical and religious thought. Although her theories often fail to emphasize the role of sadistic parents in causing justified feelings of anger within their children, her pioneering work on the relationship between anger and guilt should not be dismissed.

These examples of psychoanalytic ideas about the body and sexuality illustrate the insight that analytic theory can give about the influence of physicality on cognition and imagination. We need such insight to build theories that give realistic support for human life. We have lived through at least twenty-five hundred years of theory based on illusions of transcendent entities controlling our destinies. Whether they are called Platonic forms, Jungian archetypes, or religious deities, theories based on their existence have colluded with the denigration of physical life and of the physical environment. In order to stop disparaging the body, we might well have to give up all forms of theism and take our inspiration from ideas that see human beings as nothing more (or less) than human. We might well have to learn from theories that teach, as Rich says, that "all our high-toned questions breed in a lively animal."[44]

A Critical View of Archetypal Thinking

Jung says many different things about archetypes. Sometimes he talks about them in a low-key manner as portraits of typical ways of thinking and acting. At other times, he speaks about them in scientific terms as the images of the instincts or as invisible patterns like the electromagnetic axial systems of a crystal. Often he links his notion of archetype to Plato's theory of forms.

To make matters even more complicated, Jung's followers talk about archetypes in several other ways.[1] Some try to clarify Jung's ideas by settling on deceptively simple definitions of the term "archetype." Others focus on studies of specific images which they identify as archetypes. Still others, following the lead of James Hillman, develop an "archetypal psychology" in which images are explored and elaborated for therapeutic purposes. The archetypal psychologists sometimes prefer to use the word "image" instead of archetype. However, I would argue that they often tend to think of images in the same ways that more traditional Jungians think about archetypes.

With all these ideas about archetypes inhabiting the texts of both Jung and Jungians, it is impossible to settle on limits to the term which will do justice to every Jungian reflection on it. Further, with myriad sources available to quote, it is possible to make the word "archetype" mean just about anything you would like.[2] Nevertheless, while I cannot give you *the* definition of archetype, I can identify a specific quality of the term which pervades Jungian thought. It is a characteristic I find problematic. For me, the objectionable quality of archetypal thinking is the idea that archetypes are transcendent to the physical, human world and that they are, in part at least, not dependent on human or material contingency. Instead of directing our attention to the web of past and present social contexts which give rise to psychological phenomena, archetypal thinking draws us away from exploring our human circumstances. It leads us to imagine the influence of god-like entities such as the "Self," the "Psyche," "Eros," "Logos," "anima," and "animus." This direction in archetypal theory hampers our ability to think clearly and effectively about psychological and social problems. I'll discuss the problematic ideas I see archetypal theory producing with regard to three themes: personal therapy, empathy among social groups, and moral agency.

First, I find that in personal therapy, the idea that archetypes, images, or ancient mythologems are at work in a life instead of parents, grandparents, siblings, friends, and neighbors turns attention away from the intricate and profound ways in which we human beings structure each other's lives. Understanding your cycles of depression and anxiety as caused by biblical forces or by Greek divinities can romanticize psychological suffering but cannot unearth the roots of that suffering in your own life. The exploration of images in art and literature must be accompanied by a thoroughgoing reflection on personal history in order to be effective therapeutically. If

97

inquiry into the details of a life is neglected in favor of discussion of parallels in myths, the actual causes of psychological problems will be disguised and mystified in therapy.

Jung himself is an example of someone whose understanding of his life is hampered by archetypal thinking. I have written about how Jung mystifies his psychological difficulties in his autobiography.[3] He writes about his life in terms of encounters with theistic forces such as the dark side of God, the anima, of personalities number one and two. Instead of thinking very carefully about how he was influenced by a depressed, moody, irritable father and by an undependable mother who, he says, often lied to him and spoke "to the surrounding air," Jung attributes his deep unhappiness to impersonal forces such as a "fatal resistance to life in this world." He never seems to think about how his feelings are contingent on his particular family situation.

Because Jung could not bear to face the degree to which he was frightened and rejected by real people in his life, he developed a psychology which downplays the significance of human relationships. Jungian therapy generally places no great stress on the complexities of human emotional growth in infancy and childhood. The painful, psychological wounds within a personal history often go unnoticed and unnamed. They are rendered invisible and thus left to fester. Although the system he developed accorded Jung some emotional satisfaction and much professional success, those of us who need to understand our suffering psychologically should be wary of following his methods.

Second, I see archetypal thinking as a hindrance to empathy among social groups. This is clear from what Jung had to say about three groups of people to whom he did not belong: women, blacks, and Jews. These statements may be very difficult for those who have gained much from Jung to accept. As much as I enjoy stirring things up, I do not mean to slander Jung. My purpose here is to encourage us all to consider how archetypal thinking makes the following statements possible and insulates them from effective challenge.

About women, Jung writes:

> No one can get around the fact that by taking up a masculine profession, studying and working like a man, woman is doing something not wholly in accord with, if not directly injurious to, her feminine nature. She is doing something that would scarcely be possible for a man to do, unless he were a Chinese. Could he, for instance, be a nursemaid or run a kindergarten? When I speak of injury, I do not mean merely physiological injury, but above all psychic injury. It is a woman's outstanding characteristic that she can do anything for the love of a man. But those women who can achieve something important for the love of a *thing* are most exceptional, because this does not agree with their nature. Love for a thing is a man's prerogative.[4]

About blacks, Jung writes:

> Another thing that struck me about America was the great influence of the Negro, a psychological influence naturally, not due to the mixing of blood. . . . American music draws its main inspiration from the Negro, and so does the dance. The expression of religious feeling, the revival meetings, the Holy Rollers, and the other abnormalities are strongly influenced by the Negro, and the famous American naiveté, in its charming as well as its more unpleasant form, invites comparison with the childlikeness of the Negro. . . .
>
> This infection by the primitive can . . . be observed just as well in other countries, though not to the same degree and in this form. In Africa, for example, the white man is a diminish-

ing minority and must therefore protect himself from the Negro by observing the most rigorous social forms, otherwise he risks "going black." If he succumbs to the primitive influence he is lost. But in America the Negro, just because he is a minority, is not a degenerative influence, but rather one which, peculiar though it is, cannot be termed unfavorable—unless one happens to have a jazz phobia.[5]

About Jews, Jung writes:

The Jew, as relatively a nomad, never has produced and presumably never will produce a culture of his own, since all his instincts and gifts require a more or less civilized host-people for their development. . . . The Aryan unconscious has a higher potential than the Jewish; that is the advantage and disadvantage of a youthfulness not yet fully estranged from barbarism.[6]

In contrast to his remarks about women and blacks, these statements about Jews did get Jung into trouble in his lifetime. He was accused of being anti-Semitic by Robert Hillyer in the *Saturday Review of Literature*. Carol Baumann, an American student of Jung's, living in Switzerland, interviewed Jung about the controversy. Jung defends himself with particular reference to the two remarks quoted above:

Since this article was to be printed in Germany (in 1934) I had to write in a somewhat veiled manner, but to anyone in his senses the meaning should be clear. I had to help these people. It had to be made clear that I, an Aryan outside Germany, stood for a scientific approach to psychotherapy. That was the point! I cannot see anything in the least anti-Semitic in this statement. It is simply an appraisal of certain psychological differences in background, and in point of fact it is complimentary to the Jews to point out that they are in general more conscious and differentiated than the average Aryan, who has remained close

100

to barbarism! And it is an historical fact that the Jews have shown a remarkable ability to become carriers of the cultures in all lands wherever they have spread. This shows a high degree of civilization, and such adaptability is a matter for admiration. Some people show a funny kind of resentment when one speaks of differences in psychology—but one must admit that different nationalities and different races have different outlooks and different psychologies. Take the difference between the French and the English, or for that matter, between the English and the Americans! There is a marked difference in psychology everywhere. Only an idiot cannot see it. It is too ridiculous to be so hypersensitive about such things. They are facts of experience not to be ignored.[7]

Am I hypersensitive about such things? Being both a Jew and a woman, I do take offense at Jung's descriptions of what he terms my basic nature. I am appalled at what he says about blacks. These ideas about women, blacks, and Jews are important because instead of being peripheral to the theory Jung developed, they are, in fact, fostered by it.

I have heard Jungians argue that Jung's racist and sexist remarks are typical of the prejudices of his culture and thus should not be taken too seriously. I think this defense warrants careful attention. If we contextualize these statements in terms of the historical influences on Jung as a theorist, we begin to pull the rug out from under the notion of archetypes. By saying that Jung's thinking about blacks, Jews, and women reflects the conditions in which he lived, we recognize that what he claims to be the basic nature of women, blacks, and Jews is contingent on his own position in the world. And if we excuse Jung in this case by saying that his ideas about race and sex are the products of his times, we raise the possibility that his other ideas are also the products of his times. This line of thought can lead us to realize how all human ideas are subject to conditions. We, like Jung, are thinking with the tools of our histories.

It is important to acknowledge that when Jung tells us about his vision of women, blacks, and Jews, he does not say that this is *his* vision. He seems to feel he can talk about "women's nature," "Jewish potential," or a white's fear of "going black," as if these things are facts apparent to everyone.

Because Jung treats his own ideas as objective truths without wondering about his position as a subject, his theories do not encourage such reflection in us. Jungian theory does not lead us to investigate the webs of culture, language, and history which constructed Jung's white, male, bourgeois, Swiss Protestant vision of women, blacks, and Jews. Instead of heightening our curiosity about both the conditions which support varieties of human experience and about the conditions which structure our perceptions of human difference, instead of challenging our propensity to impute fixed natures to ourselves and to others, Jungian archetypal theory encourages closure. Archetypal thinking, at its worst, champions a language of pronouncement and decree—"women are essentially this, blacks are basically that, and Jews are what I say they are."

Archetypal thinking is not peculiar to Jungian psychology. It is present in all forms of theological and religious thought which claim to pronounce eternal and universal truths. In the West, most of the texts that support such thinking have been written by white Christian men who, like Jung, could easily deny the subjectivity of their own experience. Until very recently, white male Christian writers have worked during times in which they could assume they were looking through windows, when in fact, they were looking at mirrors. If we listen to Jung tell us how he sees blacks, Jews, and women, we hear the all-too-familiar voice of Western "man"—a being who, I believe, could become much smarter if he would become more conscious of the social context in which he theorizes.

"Myth," writes Maya Deren, "is the facts of the mind made manifest in a fiction of matter."[8] Her observation applies to archetypes as well. Archetypes are facts of mind, not of a transcendent reality. They are soft facts, conditioned facts. They change when minds change. The important thing to ask about an archetype—the question which matters most—is this: In whose mind does it exist? If an archetype exists in the minds of people with power—whether that power is political, economic, or intellectual—then that archetype can become true. People with power are able to make their dreams come true because they can create the conditions which will correspond to their sense of reality. For example, since most men have believed with Jung that women as a group are archetypically unfit for masculine professions, they have arranged domestic duties and childcare in such a way that it is unnatural (if not downright impossible) for almost any woman to study or work like a man.

Jung writes that "there are present in every psyche forms which are unconscious but nonetheless active—living dispositions, ideas in the Platonic sense, that preform and continually influence our thoughts and feelings and actions."[9] These archetypes, he thinks, "are not disseminated only by tradition, language, and migration, but . . . can rearise spontaneously, at any time, at any place, and without any outside influence."[10]

We should be critical of such a statement. If we believe that ideas can rearise spontaneously, without any outside influence, our awareness of our own responsibility is diminished. This is my third objection to archetypal thinking: it disguises human agency.

103

We live in a time when our collective capacity for destruction is threatening all life. The malfunctioning of the insecticide plant in Bhopal, India, in 1986 is but one tragedy exemplifying our grave problems. The plant released chemicals which gassed more than two thousand people. We cannot say the cause of this disaster was simply worn-out machinery or a worker's error. The chain of causation was far more complex. The plant had been built to produce insecticides which would have been unnecessary if the region's native grain were being grown on the soil. Instead, crops for export were being cultivated—crops which required a chemical shield from local insects. To understand this particular disaster, and others like it, we need to become increasingly cognizant of the implications of what we are doing, both to each other and to the environment in which we all live.

I am not digressing from the subject of archetypal theory by mentioning what happened at Bhopal. Issues such as poverty, world hunger, the arms race, and pollution of the environment should influence the way we evaluate our thinking. Comprehending the dangers we pose to both human and nonhuman life on the planet should be a central goal of the theories we build. Our situation demands that we be wary of our time-honored forms of thought and reflection because these ways of thinking might now be contributing to our problems. We need to search the inventory of philosophy, psychology, and religion to find those concepts which will let us learn more about how we have built the deep structures of our culture. We need to learn how things connect—how one part of the globe affects another part. We need to see how human presence, human action, and human behavior construct the world. We need to see these often unseen things so that we can try to change ourselves.

The notion of archetypes does not help us to see the complicated ways in which we humans affect one another. Instead of encouraging us to understand how circumstances of infancy, or of biology, or of economics, or of politics, give rise to human conditions, the theory of archetypes encourages us to settle for mystification. "Ah," we are supposed to say, "there it is again, that archetype. Let's be careful of it, give it its due, be reverent toward it. Let's not try to take it apart or reduce it to a human scale." I object to such excessive reverence because it simplifies and stupefies. To refuse to search for the material complexities, the human complexities, which produce our ideas, our visions, and our behavior is a form of reductionism which we can no longer afford. Our archetypes, our myths, our "gods" must be approached.

Roland Barthes writes this:

> One can conceive of very ancient myths, but there are no eternal ones; for it is human history which conveys reality into speech, and it alone rules the life and death of mythical language. Ancient or not, mythology can only have an historical foundation, for myth is a type of speech chosen by history; it cannot possibly evolve from the "nature of things."[11]

Barthes's words point to a direction which contemporary theory must take in order to foster the collective will to change patterns that look inevitable. We must comprehend the historical foundations of all that we are and all that we have been. We must investigate how our human agency—conscious and unconscious—has created our myths, images, and psychic structures.

There is a Buddhist teaching which states that there is really no such thing as a fire. Instead, there are only kinds of fires: wood fires, cotton fires, paper fires, etc. This teaching applies to our subject. There is no such thing as an archetype. There are, instead, only the thoughts, hopes, fears, and fantasies of particular people in their particular bodies, cultures, and histories. Just as we are in less danger of being engulfed by fires if we know the substances which fuel them, so are we safer from our human designs if we can understand the conditions which foster our ideas.

Jung was a powerful, prolific writer with a strong desire to understand both himself and his world. Knowledge of his work can help us be attentive to the imagination of our human race. But once we have learned from his teachings, we are not thereby obliged to cling to them. Another Buddhist parable advises us to treat a good teaching as we would a boat which we have used to cross a river. Once we have reached the opposite bank, we should not burden ourselves by carrying the boat overland on our backs forever. Instead, we should tie it at the shore for someone else to use. Then we should move on.

SEVEN

Body and Psyche in the Work of James Hillman

James Hillman was a major influence on my work when I was in graduate school. Preparing this essay has thus given me the occasion to return to the ideas of a mentor and to ask myself where my own thinking has gone in relation to his work—where my work is converging and where it is diverging.

When I read Hillman's works now ("*Anima Mundi,*" *Archetypal Psychology: A Brief Account, Inter Views,* and *Healing Fiction*), I find the same sparkle, the same radicalism, the same excitement that I felt when I heard Hillman deliver his Terry Lectures at Yale in 1972. I was one of the people packed into the auditorium, listening to the ideas that later became available to a much larger audience in *Revisioning Psychology.* Hillman drew the crowd he did because of a magnetism both in his prose and in his theories. Something was happening in his lectures, as he spoke about restoring a language of soul to psychology. I was at that time studying myth (what it does in the mind, how it grows in the mind), and I was fascinated with Hillman's ideas. Later, when I went to study in Zurich, I had the opportunity to work with Hillman and to watch how he was transforming traditional Jungian theory—how he was shaking up the house that Carl Jung built.

I was attracted by the iconoclasm of Hillman's work. He always took on big foes—Jungianism, psychoanalytic thought in general, religion, most contemporary psychology. Hillman's concept of the poetic basis of mind—his insistence on seeing every idea, every ideology, every mode of behavior as a fantasy and therefore as relative, contingent, conditional— presents a great method for pulling the rug out from under any set of beliefs, any dogma, any hierarchy. Archetypal psychology can assail any belief or ideology that takes itself seriously and literally with the accusation that it isn't seeing through itself, that it isn't understanding itself as a fantasy. Hillman's brand of iconoclasm—his demand that we see through ourselves and our grand ideologies is something I hope will always animate my own work.

In the past few years, my work has turned away from what I would term the "religious" psychologies, namely, Jungian and post-Jungian, to classical psychoanalysis, Freudian and post-Freudian. My old interests are still the same—myth in the mind, women in myth and the world—but I've become less and less able to mystify these topics, and I find myself increasingly interested in more materialist methods. I have begun writing about what I now see as a flight from people in our theories, and in our lives. I think there are ways in which psychoanalytic theory can address the dehumanization in the world and, I hope, help to slow it down.

Some of the work of the late Masud Khan, a British psychoanalyst, is interesting to me. Khan says "all serious thinkers—be they poets or psychologists or philosophers—in this century have been concerned about a distinct dehumanization of man's relation to himself."[1] Except for Khan's sexist language, I agree with that. I agree with him when he goes on to say that "with the Industrial Revolution and the advent of scientific technology in European cultures man began to consider himself neither in the image of God nor of man, but in that of a machine which was his own invention."[2] Khan names what I see as the theme of our times, a theme I want to take up. I want to develop theory that counters the machine fantasy of a culture in which what is efficient, reliable, fast, easy, and not alive is becoming more highly valued than any form of life, both human and nonhuman. Khan has it right, I think, when he says we are imagining ourselves to be machines. When the dominant culture is presenting this fantasy, humanists have to try very hard to stand up for what is human. At the very least, it is our job to stop despising what is human.

Hillman's work has a great deal to say on this topic. He has made, and continues to make, substantial contributions to the revitalizing of modern culture. It is here that I take much inspiration from him. I'll be more specific and focus on three of the aspects of Hillman's recent work that I find particularly vital.

First, there is Hillman's style. It is very rich and very complex, like the psyche he wants to honor. His prose is full of humor, irony, and surprise, and it thus engages us on many levels. He addresses the very human hunger for poetry, for words that move us. In *Inter Views*, Hillman says that,

> psychology has tried all century long to be scientific and now it speaks like science and is trapped in that boring language. . . . That language is clean, objective. Result: we've lost our language for describing the very material we work with—people.[3]

Modern scientific prose has become inhuman. It is written from a fantasy of distance between person and subject. It is written as if the person were a machine, something sensuously and emotionally uninvolved with what it is doing. In contrast,

Hillman is never separate from his prose—as a reader, as a listener, you always know that the man is behind the idea and that the culture and traditions of people are behind the man. Hillman, unlike so many psychologists writing today, is not trying to sound disembodied.

Second, Hillman suggests using animals as models for people. For instance, in *Inter Views,* he speaks of a cat as climbing a tree with "animal faith." He says "it loves the tree, loves itself, loves jumping and climbing—no self-examination there, no introspection about belief. Or it would stay home; or see a priest."[4] I think we would probably be better off if we saw ourselves as less spiritual and more animal. We would never expect such impossible things from animals. we would not expect them to live without enough animal warmth in the form of good food, good affection, and an appropriate environment. Also, as animals we would never underestimate our own savagery. Stressing our animality is one way of seeing what is instinctual, physical, and material about being human. Hillman's instinct is right when he begins to move toward the animal. It is a move back to basics and away from imagining ourselves as machines.

Third, Hillman examines the physical environment we are creating for ourselves. He works on understanding the *anima mundi,* that is, on seeing our world as a place ensouled. He questions the architecture, the cities, and the products that set the stage for our lives. He criticizes much of what he sees as fake, plastic, and devoid of soul and asks how authentic lives can be lived in an inauthentic environment. Since we are, as Hillman calls us, "sensuously imagining animals," we need a comfortable, sensuous environment in which to thrive.[5] We need to think about providing such an environment for the species as a whole and not just for a handful of those whom we single out as wealthy, special creatures. Theorists of the left would do well to incorporate some of Hillman's ideas on the *anima mundi* to understand better our need for physical surroundings that give inspiration as well as sustenance.

My own work with psychoanalytic theory connects with Hillman's on these general concerns about the alienation and psychological pain fostered by much of modern culture. We lose touch with what it is to be human when we imitate machines and model ourselves on that which is not alive. We also dissociate ourselves by means of certain theories and ideas that are deeply rooted in Western thought. Whenever we imagine ourselves in some fashion as controlled or directed by entities outside of ourselves—by gods, by forms, by archetypes—we distort our world and dehumanize ourselves.

Hillman offers valuable insights on this front. He objects to the belief in transcendent things that govern human life from afar. Unlike Jung, he does not separate archetypes from our imaginal experience of them. "Archetypal psychology," he says, "rigorously refuses even to speculate about a non-presented archetype *per se*."[6] He sees archetypes as "transcendent to the world of sense in their value,"[7] and not, as Jung did, in their essential nature. Hillman wants archetypal psychology to be grounded in physicality. In *Inter Views,* he says, "I am imagining an archetypal psychology that is both mythical and sensuously refined and imagistic and animal—immediate—all at once. . . . Psychoanalysis has got to take the world back into its view . . . the everyday concrete world of the senses."[8] Thus Hillman directs archetypal psychology to keep us in this world, to help us value the particular, the physical, and the sensuous. I applaud this direction. However, I see a contradiction. Dehumanization enters Hillman's philosophy with his concept of the "psyche," which takes us away

111

from people and into abstraction. For this reason, the concept warrants a critique.

D. W. Winnicott recognizes the centrality and importance of image and fantasy without deifying imagery, without abstracting images from human life and giving them a life of their own. He sees psyche as the symbols and images of the body perceived pictorially—soul is body visualized.[9] This definition seems to me most useful.

Now, by "body," I don't mean a combination of chemicals floating in a lot of water. I mean body in a psychoanalytic sense. Psychoanalysis has always moved with an understanding that bodily feelings and functions are only experienced in the context of particular bodies with particular histories. Even sex is not treated as literal genital sex. Instead, psychoanalysis sees sex as full of echoes of past feelings and past experiences. The flesh is never in a literal present but is always living in past memories and future wishes. Flesh is forever desiring, forever imaging its desires, forever remembering its past. In psychoanalysis, bodily experience is always metaphoric. "Everything physical," says Winnicott, "is imaginatively elaborated."[10]

It is this imaginative elaboration that makes life worth living, that makes culture possible, that enables relationships to give their needed warmth. Our images create bridges between our physical beings and the world outside.

In Winnicott's view, alienation from oneself or one's world occurs when the imagination fails to build bridges, when it fails to send out the pseudopodia of fantasy. This is what Hillman understands so well. He knows how much we need what he calls soul to make connections, how we need soul to live. His work urges us to feel more alive by living in the world ensouled, by living in an "enduring, intimate conversation with matter."[11] This vision in Hillman's archetypal psychology is an artistic, aesthetic, even a psychological triumph.

It might be argued that such insights about how we need images in order to live are more important than what I see as a mistaken notion of where psyche comes from. But an inhuman view of psyche is alienating in itself, especially when that view is held by practicing clinicians. A superhuman psyche draws us away from people, and it turns us away from life. Hillman teaches us that we turn away from life when we take things literally, when we stop imagining what lies behind and within our thoughts, our fantasies, our behaviors. But doesn't he fall into that same deadly literalism when he takes the psyche just as it seems, just as it presents itself to be? Doesn't archetypal psychology fail to see through itself when it fails to see psychic reality as a *contingent* reality?

The view of psychic reality as contingent is the Freudian view, and, I want to argue, it ends up being the more human, less machinelike view. In *Healing Fiction,* Hillman follows Jung in proposing that "the dream is psychic nature *per se,* unconditioned, spontaneous, primary."[12] This is in direct opposition to Freud, who always sees the dream as a melange, a kaleidoscopic vision of memories, wishes, *Tagesreste* (the day's residue), and secondary revisions. The difference of opinion on dreams becomes a difference about all of psychic reality. For Freud, the imagination is not a homogeneous, mystical entity the way it is for Jung and seems to be for Hillman. For Freud, imagination or psychic reality is a conglomeration of perceptual phenomena, contingent on all the stuff of human life. I think archetypal psychologists are misreading Freud when they interpret his discovery of the importance of fantasy to mean that he was turning away from physicality and individual history as determinants of fantasy. For Freud, psychic reality is never independent of the instinctual pressures, the historical events, and the wishful impulses that compose it. Thus, in Freudian thought, psychic reality should never be taken literally.

Freud starts psychoanalysis in the direction of deliteralizing the psyche, of seeing through psyche so that we can see more of what is human. As soon as we stop seeing through our images, motives, and ideas, we stop doing psychology and depart from what is human. Let me exaggerate a bit to make a point and suggest that Hillman depicts psyche as the machine that imagines.

The machine enters archetypal psychology when the psyche is put ahead of the human. This is a major tenet of the theory. "The human being," says Hillman in *Archetypal Psychology: A Brief Account,* "is set within the field of soul; soul is the metaphor that includes the human." [13] In *Revisioning Psychology,* he identifies psyche as the container in which everything human is placed. [14]

I suggest that when we put psyche before people both in value and in ontology, we do in psychology what we have done in technology. First, we abstract something we humans do—namely, imagine—and place the activity outside ourselves. Then we convince each other that this entity out there called "psyche" has human traits. (Archetypal psychologists assert that psyche is something that can know, feel, want, and suffer.) We begin to believe that psyche is somehow imagining us, and by believing this, we become dissociated and a bit more dehumanized.

In one sense dehumanization is a goal for Hillman. He often criticizes psychology and psychoanalysis for concentrating on the merely personal and the merely human. "A humanistic or personalistic psychology." he says, "will always fail the full perspective of soul that extends beyond human, personal behavior."[15] He believes "the Gods are *places,* and myths make place for psychic events that in an only human world become pathological."[16] I agree that things pathological are things human. But we don't cease being pathological by imagining that we are controlled from the outside. By imagining ourselves within the psyche-machine, we only avert our gaze from our own pathology. The only way to stop our destructiveness and to soothe our pain is to understand better our very, very human nature. That is why we need psychology and psychoanalysis to stay with the human, to stay wholly human.

Tom Robbins is right when he says in *Still Life with Woodpecker* that "psychology [is] at that point in its development that surgery was at when it was practiced by barbers."[17] We need to do better. Hillman is right to criticize psychology for holding trivial views of human beings, for restricting human experience, for lacking aesthetic sensibility, and for failing to have perspective on its own theories. He is right, in other words, to criticize psychology for being bad psychology, for taking poor account of people. I think he is wrong, though, to urge psychology to depart from people.[18] We need to maintain psychology as a wholly human project which aims to correct our vision if we begin to see ourselves either as gods or as machines. In order to oppose the dehumanization of people, we need to conceive psyche, not as a primary, inhuman reality, but rather as something contingent, something dependent on human experience in a physical and social world.

EIGHT

Looking at Jung Looking at Himself: A Psychoanalytic Rereading of *Memories, Dreams, Reflections*

I spent years in a Jungian universe. During that time, I read all that Carl Jung wrote and much of the work of his followers; I studied at the Jung Institute in Zürich; I had two Jungian analyses with people whom I still like a great deal. I also wrote articles about Jungian theory and taught Jungian concepts to undergraduate and graduate students. After all this, I turned away from Jungiana.

I return to write about Jung for two reasons. First, I think that the insight I now have into Jung and his thinking might be useful to people who, like me, once sought help from Jungian therapy and found it wanting. Second, I want to discuss Jung's thinking as an example of the disembodied thought I believe our Western intellectual traditions must see through and slough off.

When I first read Jung's autobiography, *Memories, Dreams, Reflections,* nearly two decades ago, I was not very familiar with Freudian and post-Freudian psychoanalytic theory. My ignorance of the psychoanalytic hermeneutic of suspicion allowed me to take Jung at his word and be thoroughly enchanted by the power and beauty of his text. Jung spoke to me as a wise, kindly, vibrant grandfather, who, even in his eighties, had a passionate interest in the depths and mysteries of human life. He appeared to be a man who had made the exploration of his psyche a lifetime adventure and who beckoned every reader to do the same. He moved me deeply. I was inspired to go to Zürich and enter Jungian analysis.

It was my interest in Jungian thinking that eventually led me to study psychoanalysis. In order to understand Jung better, I started to read certain works of Freud, such as *The Interpretation of Dreams,* for which Jung had expressed appreciation. My work with things Freudian and post-Freudian (such as object relations theory) leads me to rethink my approach to Jung. Now, when I return to *Memories* with a perspective derived from psychoanalysis, I see another Jung emerge from the text. Alongside the man who deeply wanted to understand himself, I see one who never looked clearly at the human factors involved in the etiology of his own suffering. Jung's unwillingness or inability to consider the influence of his family on his own pain explains, I think, why he developed a psychology which both largely ignores childhood and attributes emotional difficulties to the workings of abstract, inhuman forces.[1]

To explore this idea, I will concentrate on the first three chapters of *Memories, Dreams, Reflections,* titled "First Years," "School Years," and "Student Years." According to Aniela Jaffé, who recorded Jung's words and edited the entire text, Jung wrote these chapters by himself, in the winter of 1958. "After a period of inner turbulence," writes Jaffé, "long-submerged images out of his childhood rose to the surface of his mind. One morning he informed me that he wanted to set down his recollections of his childhood directly. . . . In April

117

1958, Jung finished the three chapters on his childhood, school days, and years at the university."[2] Thus, by focusing on the first three chapters of *Memories,* I can be certain I am using material which represents Jung's mature and careful reflections on his own life.[3]

Jung says he had to overcome much internal resistance to write about his childhood. "The task," he says, "has proved so difficult and singular that in order to go ahead with it, I have had to promise myself that the results would not be published in my lifetime. Such a promise seemed to me essential in order to assure for myself the necessary detachment and calm" (p. viii). In fact, Jung writes that for much of his life he placed great value on not disclosing anything about the dreams and fantasies which had made the greatest impression on him. For instance, until he was sixty-five, he did not mention anything about the dream he identifies as the most important one he ever had. "A strict taboo hung over all these matters, inherited from my childhood," he says. "I could never have talked about them with friends. . . . My entire youth can be understood in terms of this secret [of the dreams and visions]. It induced in me an almost unendurable loneliness. My one great achievement during those years was that I resisted the temptation to talk about it with anyone" (p. 41).

Considering that Jung was a practicing analyst for over fifty years, it is remarkable that he would set such store in keeping his own important memories so secret.[4] I also find it surprising that Jung would stress that, even as an old man, he still had not understood his early life. "To this day," he says, "writing down my memories at the age of eighty-three, I have never fully unwound the tangle of my earliest memories" (p. 27). When I first read these words years ago, I took them to be simply an expression of Jung's honesty in admitting the

118

limits of psychological understanding. Now I wonder why it was that Jung's childhood remained such a mystery to him, and I question the merits of a psychology which, after being practiced for a lifetime, left its founder so puzzled about his own early mental life.

There is no doubt that Jung had a difficult childhood. As a small boy, he suffered from anxiety at night, general eczema, coughing fits, and fainting spells. He recalls what he describes as "overwhelming images" of a painful fall and two deep cuts on his leg and head. He remembers being told that as a child he tried to throw himself off a bridge into a waterfall. The bruises and this near catastrophe, he says, point to "an unconscious suicidal urge or, it may be, to a fatal resistance to life in this world" (p. 9).

This "resistance" to living seems to be related to an unspecified but powerful fear Jung had of enjoying what the world had to offer him. When he started grade school, he says, the world seemed "hostile," "in some obscure way." He continues the thought: "Though I became increasingly aware of the beauty of the bright daylight world where 'golden sunshine filters through green leaves,' at the same time I had a premonition of the inescapable world of shadows filled with frightening, unanswerable questions which had me at their mercy" (p. 19). This tendency to shrink back from the world characterized his years at school. Jung speaks of a "physical timidity" which was "linked with a distrust of the world and its potentialities. To be sure, the world seemed to me beautiful and desirable, but it was also filled with vague and incomprehensible perils" (p. 29).

As a young adolescent, Jung writes that he had a "fitful appetite" and was in "unstable health" (p. 76). He remembers being "shy, timid and mistrustful" (p. 70), but at fifteen being

119

"prone to violent rages" (p. 44). He says his mother told him he was often depressed during the years of puberty. But instead of saying that early adolescence was a sad time for him, Jung prefers to describe his moodiness as "brooding on the secret" of one of his visions (p. 42). As a teenager, however, he does describe himself as being depressed, or rather, as being led into depressions "in increasing measure" by what he calls his "No. 2 personality" (p. 63).

Taken all together, these depressions, fears, rages, and physical ailments indicate that Jung grew up in troubled circumstances. However, in his efforts to understand his psychological turbulence, he searches for few links between his parents' behavior and his own considerable difficulties. Instead, he prefers to regard his childhood experiences as evidence that mysterious, abstract, divine forces were at work in his psyche. This tendency to downplay the influence of his parents on his emotional life is evident throughout *Memories, Dreams, Reflections*. A striking example is Jung's discussion of an important dream he had between the ages of three and four.

This dream, Jung says, "was to preoccupy me all my life." He relates it in detail:

> The vicarage stood quite alone near Laufen castle, and there was a big meadow stretching back from the sexton's farm. In the dream I was in this meadow. Suddenly I discovered a dark, rectangular, stone-lined hole in the ground. I had never seen it before. I ran forward curiously and peered down into it. Then I saw a stone stairway leading down. Hesitantly and fearfully, I descended. At the bottom was a doorway with a round arch, closed off by a green curtain. It was a big, heavy curtain of worked stuff like brocade, and it looked very sumptuous. Curious to see what might be hidden behind, I pushed it aside. I saw before me in the dim light a rectangular chamber about thirty feet long. The ceiling was arched and of hewn stone. The

floor was laid with flagstones, and in the center a red carpet ran from the entrance to a low platform. On this platform stood a wonderfully rich golden throne. I am not certain, but perhaps a red cushion lay on the seat. It was a magnificent throne, a real king's throne in a fairy tale. Something was standing on it which I thought at first was a tree trunk twelve to fifteen feet high and about one and a half to two feet thick. It was a huge thing, reaching almost to the ceiling. But it was of a curious composition: it was made of skin and naked flesh, and on top there was something like a rounded head with no face and no hair. On the very top of the head was a single eye, gazing motionlessly upward.

It was fairly light in the room, although there were no windows and no apparent source of light. Above the head, however, was an aura of brightness. The thing did not move, yet I had the feeling that it might at any moment crawl off the throne like a worm and creep toward me. I was paralyzed with terror. At that moment I heard from outside and above me my mother's voice. She called out, "Yes, just look at him. That is the man-eater!" That intensified my terror still more, and I awoke sweating and scared to death. For many nights afterward I was afraid to go to sleep, because I feared I might have another dream like that. (pp. 11–12)

The image of the huge, fleshy underground thing "haunted" Jung "for years." He writes that "only much later did I realize that what I had seen was a phallus." "Decades" after this initial insight, Jung says that he understood that it was a "ritual phallus." Instead of describing the organ in the dream as erect, he says that it had "abstract significance," which "is shown by the fact that it was enthroned by itself ithyphallically," a word whose Greek root, meaning "upright," Jung explains in a parenthesis (p. 12).

Jung does not wonder whether the eye of the phallus could indicate something which his own eye might have seen. "At all events," he says, "the phallus of this dream seems to be a subterranean God 'not to be named,' and it remained such throughout my youth" (p. 13). He does not even mention the possibility that, as a little boy, he might well have been both very interested in and very frightened by glimpses of his father's erect penis. "I do not know where the anatomically correct phallus could have come from," he writes some eighty years after the dream (ibid.). The thought that his father's organ (or, indeed, his own) might have had some connection with the male genital in his dream, seems never to have crossed his mind.[5]

Although he does not link the dream with any actual event in his life, Jung places it in a year that was traumatic for him. He had the dream the same year in which his parents underwent a temporary separation and in which his mother was hospitalized for "several months" in Basel. "Presumably," Jung writes, "her illness had something to do with the difficulty in the marriage." "Dim intimations of trouble in my parents' marriage hovered around me," he remembers. Jung was upset by his mother's absence, as would be any young child. "I was deeply troubled by my mother's being away," he says (p. 8).

Jung connects his parents' separation to the eczema that made him feverish and unable to sleep. But surprisingly, he does not link either the separation or his mother's disappearance to the fear he had felt in his dream, a "terror" which, he says, had become "intensified" when he heard his mother's voice at a distance, "outside" and "above." The only question which Jung says he has about his mother's presence in the dream is how the words of her warning should be inflected. He writes: "I could never make out whether my mother meant, '*That* is the man-eater,' or 'That is the *man-eater*' " (p. 12). I suggest that Jung's worry about linguistics displaces his confusion about the dream onto something rather trivial. The central imagery of the dream and the power it exerted for a lifetime certainly seem to arise from Jung's deep anxieties about his parents. It is the source of these anxieties which Jung seems unable to approach.

Even though Jung's concern about his mother's exact phrasing seems to be a diversion, his associations to the word "man-eater" are important. Jung explains:

> In the first case [i.e., "*That* is the man-eater."], she would have meant that not Lord Jesus or the Jesuit was the devourer of little children, but the phallus; in the second case [i.e. "That is the *man-eater*"], that the "man-eater" in general was symbolized by the phallus, so that the dark Lord Jesus, the Jesuit, and the phallus were identical. (p. 12)

In previous pages, Jung has said he had been frightened when he saw a Catholic priest dressed in a black robe walking over the hilltop near his house. He identifies the priest with the word "Jesuit," a term which he knew provoked strong reactions among the Protestant clergymen of his own family. Jung explains that the name "Jesuit" was particularly frightening to him because it sounded very like the "Jesus" who was said to "take" dead people to himself when they were buried. This image of Lord Jesus as a "god of death," says Jung, was reinforced by a prayer his mother had taught him to say every night—a prayer that seemed to imply Jesus might devour little children (pp. 10–11).

Jung's misunderstanding of the rhyme is a central reason he gives for suspecting that Jesus devoured people and put them in holes in the ground. The Jungian analyst Marie-Louise von Franz agrees: "Through a misunderstanding of a child's prayer, which he was taught, he came gradually to the conviction that Jesus was a 'maneater.'"[6] Although von Franz, in jar-

123

gon all too characteristic of Jungian studies, mentions other possible causes for this morbidity, such as "a psychic atmosphere in which religious faith had lost its original living quality and had to a large extent rigidified into a collective-conscious life-style," neither she nor anyone else reflects on the particular tragedy which might well have been relevant to Jung's fear.[7] An older brother had died two years before Jung's birth. Paul Jung, the father's namesake, had lived only for a couple of days.[8]

It is interesting to speculate whether Jung's parents had ever mentioned his dead predecessor to young Carl. If they had, they very likely would have explained his brother's fate in the same manner that Jung says they explained the deaths of other people. "Certain persons," writes Jung, "who had been around previously would suddenly no longer be there. Then I would hear that they had been buried, and that Lord Jesus had taken them to himself" (p. 9). If Jung had known about his dead brother, he would have had more reason to be afraid he too might die and wind up in a hole with the fearsome Lord Jesus. Further, his mother, Emilie, might have feared that Carl could die just as suddenly as young Paul had. This could have been why she taught Carl to recite the nightly protective prayer he found so scary. In any case, the influence of the infant Paul's death both on the parents and on the brother warrants more attention than it has so far received.

In the discussion of the dream of the phallus, there is another, less speculative instance of how Jung avoids linking his psychological experience to the influence of the people closest to him. Although he does see a web of connections within the morbid religious imagery underlying his dream, he fails to join the images to any feelings about his parents. Jung writes that the subterranean phallic God not to be named "reap-

124

peared" throughout his youth "whenever anyone spoke too emphatically about Lord Jesus." The Christian doctrine he had been taught, he says, "often . . . seemed to me a solemn masquerade, a kind of funeral at which the mourners put on serious or mournful faces but the next moment were secretly laughing and not really sad at all" (p. 13). And, although the Jesus he invoked each night in his prayer helped to scare away "the terrors of the night," Jung tended to see him as "a god of death," "uncanny," and "a crucified and bloody corpse" (ibid.). Christ's love and kindness were doubtful to him, he explains, "because the people who talked most about 'dear Lord Jesus' wore black frock coats and shiny black boots which reminded me of burials." These people were, he remembers, "my father's colleagues as well as eight of my uncles—all parsons. For many years they inspired fear in me—not to speak of occasional Catholic priests who reminded me of the terrifying Jesuit" (ibid.). Why, I wonder, does Jung not include the parson Paul Jung among these men? Obviously his father was the clergyman Jung knew best.

Jung must have heard his father mention Jesus at the local funerals at which he officiated. Jung's memories of these rituals are vivid. "People drowned," he writes,

> bodies were swept over the rocks. In the cemetery nearby, the sexton would dig a hole—heaps of brown, upturned earth. Black solemn men in long frock coats and unusually tall hats and shiny black boots would bring a black box. My father would be there in his clerical gown, speaking in a resounding voice. Women wept. I was told that someone was being buried in this hole in the ground. (p. 9)

This description of the role his father played at burials suggests the setting of Jung's dream—a "hole in the ground."

125

Jung, however, never seems to be conscious of how his recollection of his father's duties at funerals could be at all relevant either to the imagery of the dream that obsessed him all his life or to his suspicions about Christian clerics and their connections with death.

Jung's silence about Paul Jung in his explanation of the dream is significant. How could his father *not* have had anything to do with his childhood notions about the scariness of the clergy and their doctrines? How could his father have had nothing to do with the dream image of a large terrifying phallus? Jung's refusal to mention his father in close connection with his childhood ideas about Christianity and death indicates that, even at the age of eighty-one, he was denying the degree of resentment he harbored toward his father.

The ambivalence and fear which are basic to the dream Jung had at age four also structure a famous vision about God he had in early adolescence. The images of this revelation are, I think, an expression both of the deep rage Jung felt toward his father and of his desire to triumph over the things his father represented. When he was twelve, Jung was plagued for days by a troubling thought which he felt was just at the border of consciousness. The troublesome idea, he says, was somehow connected with his appreciation of the beautiful cathedral in his town square. One fine summer day, he writes, he had been "overwhelmed" by the loveliness of the building in the sunshine. But just as he was enjoying the tranquility of the scene, he was overcome with a choking sensation and felt he must stop himself from thinking something horrible. He was able to stave off the thought for several days (p. 36).[9]

Up until the moment he allowed himself to think the thought through to the end, he was aware of feeling very guilty. He had the urge to confess what was on his mind.

126

"But," he writes, "I resisted the temptation to confess, aided by the thought that it would cause my parents intense sorrow" (p. 37).

Finally, however, Jung allowed himself to continue his train of thought. "I gathered all my courage," he writes, "as though I were about to leap forthwith into hell-fire, and let the thought come. I saw before me the cathedral, the blue sky. God sits on His golden throne, high above the world—and from under the throne an enormous turd falls upon the sparkling new roof, shatters it, and breaks the walls of the cathedral asunder" (p. 39).

Jung says that immediately after this vision he felt "an enormous, indescribable relief." He marvels that "the wisdom and goodness of God had been revealed to me now that I had yielded to His inexorable command." This new knowledge, he felt, was unavailable to his father. "That was what my father had not understood," Jung writes,

> he failed to experience the will of God, had opposed it for the best reasons and out of the deepest faith. And that was why he had never experienced the miracle of grace which heals all and makes all comprehensible. He had taken the Bible's commandments as his guide; he believed in God as the Bible prescribed and as his forefathers had taught him. But he did not know the immediate living God who stands, omnipotent and free, above His Bible and His Church. (p. 40)

It is no wonder Jung finds this vision so delightful. First, the imagery expressed his inner wish to "shit" on his father, who was so closely associated with Church structures. Second, it insulated him from feeling guilty about his wickedness by assuring him that the shit was heaven-sent and that it signified a special relationship he had with God. The vision meant that

127

Carl, the son, and not Paul, the father, was God's real confidant.[10]

Although in his fantasy, Jung was gloriously triumphant
over his father, he remained uneasy about the aggression he
felt toward Paul Jung.[11] Soon after he had the vision, he says,
"Church became a place of torment" (p. 45). He would sit at
services feeling very doubtful and uneasy when he heard his
father's emotional sermons praising the "good God." "Does
he really know what he is talking about?" the young Jung
wonders. "Could he have me, his son, put to the knife as a
human sacrifice, like Isaac, or deliver him to an unjust court
which would have him crucified like Jesus?" (pp. 46–47).

Jung says he decided that his father could not "do that," but
he was still obsessed with the idea that "He [God] could be
terrible" and with the images of biblical fathers' cruelty to
their sons (ibid.). This indicates that, at some level, Jung was
very worried about paternal violence. His last great theoretical
treatise, *Answer to Job,* which was completed just before he began serious work on *Memories,* centers on the same theme.

In her introduction to *Memories,* Aniela Jaffé observes that
one of the reasons Jung was interested in working on his autobiography was that he "sensed" that the recollections of his
childhood had a "connection with ideas he had written in his
old age." "But," she adds, "he could not grasp it clearly" (p.
vi). If we compare Jung's account of his early memories with
Answer to Job, I think we can begin to solve the puzzle. In *Job,*
Jung is concerned with God's sadism toward his children. He
discusses the theological problem posed by the cruelty God
showed first toward Job and later, Jesus. He chides theologians for the cowardly ways in which they try to avoid confront-
ing the evil that lurks in the biblical Father.[12]

Jung claims that Job and Jesus both understood that the
divine Father has a very dark side. He interprets Christ's

scream on the cross—"My God, my God, why have you forsaken me?"—as an acknowledgment of the Father's complicity in the son's murder.[13] He also calls attention to a request Jesus made of God in the Lord's Prayer. Why, asks Jung, would Jesus petition God to "lead us not into temptation" if he did not already have some conviction about the untrustworthiness of the Almighty?[14]

In *Answer to Job,* Jung both identifies a central problem in theology and inadvertently reveals more about his own psychology. I am not suggesting that the text of *Memories* indicates that Jung was *merely* projecting his worries about his father onto the stories of Job and Jesus. However, I do think that Jung's incentive to explore the "shadow" of God in the Old and New Testaments is his desire to approach the violence of the imagery which had plagued him from childhood. If we juxtapose *Answer to Job* with the first three chapters of *Memories,* we can see Jung struggling with the same issue in both texts, namely, how can a son—Job, Jesus, or Carl—cope with a father's ill-will?

Since Jung never wants to see his parents as central causes of his childhood misery, he searches for divine agents behind the psychological dramas he watched within himself. In *Memories,* he writes:

> I asked myself: "Who talks like that? Who has the impudence to exhibit a phallus so nakedly, in a shrine? Who makes me think that God destroys His Church in this abominable manner?" At last I asked myself whether it was not the devil's doing. For that it must have been God or the devil who spoke and acted in this way was something I never doubted. (p. 47)[15]

That Paul Jung must have been at least as relevant to these thoughts as God or the devil is something Jung could not admit.

The early chapters of *Memories* are suffused with Jung's indirect statements that he felt something was seriously amiss with his father throughout his childhood. These statements become visible if we avoid the particularly Jungian trap of using abstract, archetypal forces to explain human psychology. By Jung's own account, he had always been a witness to his parents' marital disputes and to his father's bursts of temper. At the age of three, he says he had "intimations" of trouble in his parents' marriage (p. 8). Since these intimations were soon followed by his mother's hospitalization for several months, young Carl might have felt that his father had sent his mother away. This early impression of his father as dangerous (like the "man-eater" in his dream) could have been reinforced in the years that followed. In later adolescence, Jung mentions that "angry scenes" occurred between his parents "only too frequently." He adds that he would remain passive during his father's "outbursts of rage" (pp. 91–92). If, as seems to be the case, discord was typical of Jung's experience from the time he was a toddler until he was in his twenties, it might well explain much about the turbulence of his fantasies. Concern for making peace between his warring parents might also be reflected in Jung's avid interest in mystical systems which strive for a *coniunctio oppositorum* (union of the opposites).

When Jung was twenty-one, Paul Jung died of an intestinal ailment which had likely been causing him pain for a long time. Jung writes that "for a number of years he had complained of all sorts of abdominal symptoms." Ill health might well have been one of the determinants of the depression, "hypochondria," and "moody irritability," which Jung lists as characteristics of his father (pp. 25, 94). Perhaps, particularly when Jung was a child, his father's depression, anger, and unhappiness might have given Jung the impression that physical violence was possible. Indeed, it is not out of the question to wonder whether some physical abuse might have actually occurred.

As unlikely as it might seem, the possibility that Carl was sexually assaulted by his father cannot be ruled out. In 1907, in a letter to Freud, Jung says that he had been a victim of sexual assault by a man he once "worshiped."[16] This is why, he explains, he found his closeness with Freud so problematic. Could the man to whom Jung refers have been a relative? Was the abuse repeated over a period of time? The answers to these questions are important.

Jung did exhibit three traits which often characterize children who have been sexually abused by a parent or close relative:

1. From early childhood, he harbored a deep anger toward one parent, his father.

2. As a child, he fashioned an image of a little man, hid it away from his family, and cherished it. Jung kept this manikin in a pencil case in the attic, where he fed it and wrote it messages in a secret script. The doll gave him the great comfort of knowing he had something "no one could get at." "It was an inviolable secret which must never be betrayed," he writes, "for the safety of my life depended on it" (p. 22). From accounts of survivors of incest, we know that the technique of imaginatively splitting off a part of oneself to keep it safe is often employed as a way of maintaining sanity.

3. He had a penchant for seducing his patients. Sabina Spielrein and Toni Wolff are the best known examples of women with whom Jung transgressed the role of doctor.[17] Perhaps having sex with some of his patients was one way Jung mimicked the improper attentions he himself had received as a child.

131

I realize the seriousness of suggesting that a family member might have perpetrated the abuse to which Jung refers in the letter. Nevertheless, there is sufficient reason to warrant exploring the hypothesis further with more research on the Jung family.[18] I agree with Henri Ellenberger, the historian of psychoanalysis, that "we do not know enough about the personality of Reverend Paul Jung to understand the reason for the strong resentment that his son felt toward him during his whole life."[19]

Carl identifies Paul Jung's religious doubts as the prime causes of the man's deep unhappiness (p. 93). It was these doubts which, he says, communicated themselves to him as a child and caused his unconscious to react with its own "'religious' ideas" (p. 90). But this reasoning is too vague and intellectualized to take account of things such as his dream at age four or his vision at age twelve. Rather than Paul Jung's "doubts," surely it was his angry behavior and emotional anguish which Jung imbibed as a young child. While it is not unlikely that doubt about his vocation was part of Paul Jung's problems, Jung's tendency to give this as the major reason for the discontent in the household was a way of avoiding a closer look at his father's unhappiness. Likewise, writing that his father was "usually irritable" because "he did a great deal of good" is a poor attempt at accounting for Paul Jung's angry moods (p. 91). When Jung writes that "theology had alienated my father and me from one another" (p. 93), he is ignoring the long-term emotional and psychological estrangement which found expression in their heated intellectual disputes.[20]

Masud Khan uses the term "cumulative trauma" to refer to a psychological condition caused by either a succession of traumatic incidents over time or by a persistent atmosphere of emotional strain.[21] I find this a useful notion to apply to Jung's account of his own life. Rather than look for one major event to explain Jung's violent fantasies, we can understand his suffering as the cumulative result of living with two deeply troubled people—Paul Jung and Emilie Preiswerk Jung.

Jung writes more openly about his mother's failings than he does about those of his father. Nevertheless, although he seems more conscious of his mother's faults, he does shrink from acknowledging the full implications of her pathology. The followers of Jung unintentionally collude in downplaying Emilie Jung's problems by describing her in a clichéd fashion as an eccentric, earthy woman with intimations of deep, pagan wisdom. At the annual Jung conference at Notre Dame, I once heard Laurens van der Post smilingly refer to Jung's mother as "a bit of a witch."[22] Such labeling functions as a way of dismissing Emilie Jung's considerable peculiarities.

It is difficult to find a paragraph Jung writes about his mother that does not take a negative turn. Often Jung's comments about his mother simply trivialize her. He says that "in conversation she was not adequate for me" and that "her chatter was like the gay plashing of a fountain" (p. 48). He takes a slightly more serious tone when he recalls how embarrassed she made him feel by loudly calling out humiliating instructions when he left the house (p. 26).

These frequent, relatively minor criticisms take on some importance in the context of other things Jung says about Emilie Jung. In both the autobiography and in published interviews, Jung continually alludes to the disappointment he felt about his mother's care of him. He also seems to have been suspicious about her mental health. These problems began for him at a young age.

By the time he reached the age of three, Jung had come to cherish a person who substituted for his mother. He states that "the whole essence of womanhood" was symbolized by a maid who, along with an aunt, had cared for him when his mother was hospitalized (p. 9). "I still remember," he writes in his eighties,

> her picking me up and laying my head against her shoulder. She had black hair and an olive complexion, and was quite different from my mother. I can see, even now, her hairline, her throat, with its darkly pigmented skin, and her ear. . . . It was as though she belonged not to my family but only to me. (p. 8)

It was this maid, he says, who was responsible for saving his life when, as a small child, he tried to throw himself over a bridge (p. 90).

In contrast to the maid, Jung tells us that his mother was often undependable. From the time of his mother's hospital stay, he writes that he "felt mistrustful when the word 'love' was spoken." After her absence, he says that for a long time he associated the word "woman" with a feeling of "innate unreliability" (p. 8).

One reason for Jung's sense that he could not depend on his mother was her habit of staying in bed. Jung writes that his "mother's invalidism" as well as his "father's irritability" "oppressed" him (p. 21). In the time before the birth of his sister, he writes that he had noticed nothing different about his mother since he was not at all surprised at "my mother's lying in bed more frequently than usual." He says he considered her taking to bed "an inexcusable weakness" in any case (p. 25).

Jung drops several hints about noticing Emilie Jung's strange behavior. When he disbelieved the stork story that his

134

parents told him about his sister's birth, Jung says he interpreted this obvious lie as an attempt to conceal the fact that "my mother had once again done something I was supposed not to know about." Further, he mentions that his "sense of distrust" about Johanna Jung's sudden appearance was validated by "subsequent odd reactions on the part of my mother." Whatever this behavior was, Jung writes that it "confirmed my suspicions that something regrettable was connected with this birth" (p. 25).

What were these things his mother did that Jung was "supposed not to know about"? Did she do something to make him feel she herself regretted the birth of Johanna Jung? Are Jung's remarks simply to be dismissed as memories of the jealousy he felt when his sister was born? Or is he saying something further about Emilie Jung's confusing behavior toward both her children? Other statements that Jung makes about his mother give some evidence that the latter is true.

In a famous BBC television interview, Jung speaks in general terms about problems with his mother. John Freeman, the interviewer, asks, "Which did you get on with more intimately—your father or your mother?" "That's difficult to say," Jung replies. "Of course, one is always more intimate with the mother, but when it comes to the personal feeling I had a better relation to my father, who was predictable, than with my mother, who was to me a very problematical something."[23] Considering all the difficulties Jung had with his father, his idea that his mother was even more problematic is indeed surprising. A bit further on in their conversation, Jung says that his mother frightened him. "I realized that I had fear of my mother," he tells Freeman, "but not during the day. Then she was quite known to me and predictable, but in the night I had fear of my mother." When Freeman pursues this disclosure by asking, "And can you remember why?" Jung answers, "I have not the slightest idea."[24]

Similarly, in *Memories,* Jung recalls being afraid of his mother. "As a child I often had anxiety dreams about her," he writes. "By day she was a loving mother, but at night she seemed uncanny" (p. 50). But in *Memories,* unlike in the interview, Jung does give a reason for fearing Emilie Jung—namely, that she had two personalities. "At night," he writes, she seemed "like one of those seers who is at the same time a strange animal, like a priestess in a bear's cave . . . archaic and ruthless; ruthless as truth and nature" (ibid.).

In a few other passages in the autobiography, Jung mentions being terrified by his mother's tendency to change into her "unconscious" personality. "That personality," he says, was "unexpectedly powerful—a somber, imposing figure possessed of unassailable authority and no bones about it." When "this other" came out, he writes, "it was unexpected and frightening . . . [then] she would speak as if talking to herself, but what she said was aimed at me and usually struck to the core of my being, so that I was stunned into silence" (pp. 48–49). Using other words to describe the same fear, he says, "when her second personality burst forth, what she said on those occasions was so true and to the point that I trembled before it" (p. 52). Such statements indicate Emilie Jung might have said hurtful things to Carl when she was under the influence of her number two personality. Although he criticizes her for admiring him too much, his use of words such as "ruthless" to describe the truth his mother "aimed" at the core of his being, imply that she was cruel when "the other" emerged. In any case, whether or not she was particularly unkind when she was transformed, the fact that she radically changed her

136

nature "now and then" was surely enough to explain Jung's alarm at his mother's number two personality (p. 49).

To most psychologists, a mother who terrifies her small son by adopting a second personality would be regarded as a likely threat to the mental health of her offspring. Jung, however, never gives his mother's instability the attention it merits. Instead, just like many young children who cannot admit the madness of a parent, he pretends that his mother's habit of changing personalities was actually quite acceptable. He even manages to see an advantage in her condition because her "number two personality" gave her a particular kind of wisdom (p. 50). In what must have been a small boy's attempt to identify with his mother, Jung insists that as a child, he had a number two personality also. How Jung coped with this other personality is a major theme of the early chapters of his autobiography. Although, he says that "number two" offered him "peace and solitude," he also writes that it frequently led him into depressions (pp. 45, 63). I suggest that coping with his mother's episodes of dissociation was an important, but never mentioned, component of his own struggle for sanity.

Besides fearing his mother's personality changes, Jung also worried that Emilie Jung was a liar. By the time he was eleven, Jung says his mother had made him her "confidant" by telling him "everything she could not say to my father." One day she told him something particularly disturbing—something that Jung says "concerned my father and alarmed me greatly." He was extremely upset and went off to consult with a man whom he thought could help. When Jung returned home after failing to meet the man, he discovered that his mother was now saying something very different. He felt stupid and was glad that the "influential person" had not been at home. He writes that "it was by the mercy of providence that he was not there."

From then on, his confidence in his mother was "strictly limited." He tells us, "I decided to divide everything my mother said by two" (p. 52).

In addition to revealing how much Jung distrusted his mother, this incident also suggests that Emilie Jung might have encouraged tensions between father and son. How could the intimate confidences she shared with Carl rather than Paul not have been a major influence on the son's sense of superiority over the father? Although Jung says, when writing about the vision of shit on the cathedral, that at the age of twelve he felt it was God who had revealed things to him that his father did not understand, in reality, it was his mother who was telling him special secrets. This situation is likely to have fueled Jung's rage both against his father for rejecting his mother and against his mother for burdening him with such exciting but intrusive intimacy.

It is no wonder that the fantasies Jung remembers having at this time in his life concerned protecting hidden treasures and fortifying medieval castles (pp. 80–82).[25] In early adolescence, he must have felt he needed an enormous amount of strength and cunning to protect himself from being crushed by the considerable psychological burdens his parents were forcing him to carry.

Years later, when Jung's father died, Emilie Jung seems to have been eager to have her son assume some of her husband's functions. Jung writes that one day after his father's death—a death which, Jung says, he was "fascinated" to watch—his mother, "in her 'second' voice," said to him, "or to the surrounding air," that "he died in time for you." Jung interprets her figuratively to mean that "you did not understand each other and he might have become a hindrance to you"—a view which, he says, "fit in with my mother's No. 2 personality."

However, his newly widowed mother very literally put Jung in his father's place. He moved into Paul Jung's room and had to give her the housekeeping money because, explains Jung, "she was unable to economize and could not manage money" (p. 96). Although Jung does not make the connection, we can see that the role of husband-substitute which Jung's mother gave him to play after his father's death was similar to the one in which she had cast him at the age of eleven.

After reading Jung's autobiography with attention to the kind of details I have discussed here, it becomes difficult to accept his own explanations about the great influence that archetypes and divinities had in his life. Paul and Emilie, rather than God and the devil, were the major actors. Furthermore, focusing on the things Jung says about his parents also sheds some light both on the relationships he had as an adult and on some of the major themes of his theories.

For example, we know that relationships with older male mentor figures were hard for Jung to maintain. Flournoy, Bleuler, and Janet were all teachers whom Jung eventually found disappointing.[26] However, it was Sigmund Freud who overshadowed these men as Jung's most illustrious failed father figure. On their trip to America, Freud suggested that Jung's dream of two skulls revealed the death wishes Jung felt toward him. Jung's denial of this suggestion was vehement (pp. 159–160). Perhaps his refusal to consider the possibility that he felt aggression toward the older man was reminiscent of the way he denied the anger he felt toward his father.[27]

Jung's habits regarding women might also have their roots in the troubles of his childhood. Jung seemed to need and appreciate women as helpers and collaborators. Yet despite his intimacy with women, he was careful to keep his distance from any one woman by maintaining several relationships at once.

139

His decades-long triangular arrangement with his wife, Emma Jung, and his friend, Toni Wolff, is the most well-known example. However, by many accounts, Jung seems to have also cultivated an intellectual harem among those women who were never his lovers. I remember Aniela Jaffé remarking that Jung would often make a women with whom he talked "feel like the queen of heaven." But eventually, she said, "you would find out there were other queens of heaven."[28]

Jung's practice of distributing his affections among several women should not be dismissed simply as a consequence of his roguish disposition. Nor should it be spiritualized, as he sometimes did, as the typical search of the "complicated" middle-aged man for psychic "wholeness."[29] When we know how undependable and even frightening Jung found his mother to be, we can, I think, understand why Jung could never let himself depend very heavily on any one woman.[30] Although Emilie Jung had brought him up feeling special because she shared secrets with him, she also had taught him to mistrust her profoundly. In later life, he seemed to have retained a need for women's intense conversation along with a deep suspicion of their motives.

In a widely published interview held close to the end of his life, Jung says, "to me a particularly beautiful woman is a source of terror. A beautiful woman is as a rule a terrible disappointment; you cannot have your cake and eat it."[31] Perhaps this feeling applied in some degree to all the women with whom Jung was close, to all those from whom he derived nourishment. On some level they all seemed like his mother—interesting but also terrifying and unreachable. He thus always needed to balance them against each other as a way of minimizing the inevitable disappointment.

I think we can also see Emilie Jung's effect on her son in his choice of subjects to study. Scholars of psychoanalysis have remarked that while Freud began his work by studying hysterics, Jung's first concern was schizophrenics. Even though this difference was certainly influenced by the patients whom each man was sent,[32] in Jung's case, his sustained interest in schizophrenic phenomena could very likely have been fueled by the troubles he had with his mother. His intense childhood wish to understand and thus not be frightened by his mother's personality changes found expression in later life in his desire to comprehend schizophrenics.[33] His remarkable ability to talk with very disturbed people and even find them charming might well have been fostered by his dealings with his mother's "number two."[34]

Emilie Jung's plural personality might also have come alive for Jung in theology. In *Memories,* directly after explaining how he doubted everything his mother told him and how he "trembled before" her "second personality," he writes about how fascinated he was when he saw God's multiple selves mentioned in the book of catechism he was studying with his father. "I came across the paragraph on the Trinity," he remembers. "Here was something that challenged my interest: a oneness which was simultaneously a threeness. This was a problem that fascinated me because of its inner contradiction. I waited long for the moment when we would reach this question" (pp. 52–53). By recalling this theological subject directly after writing a rather lengthy reflection on his mother's plural nature, Jung inadvertently suggests that, in his mind, the triple God and the double Emilie were linked. Likewise, Jung's conviction that God had a "dark side" might well have been linked with the "ruthless nature" Jung says he saw emerge in Emilie Jung's "number two" moments. Like his father's "moody irritability," his mother's twoness gave him reason to doubt the benevolence of any parental figure.

This psychoanalytic approach to what Jung says about himself shows that he had ample reason to find the atmosphere in his childhood home "unbreathable" (p. 19) and to feel himself in opposition to "life" (p. 9). His sense of self-worth was probably influenced by the undependable affections of both his parents. Their odd moods and rejecting behavior could explain why he wondered whether he might possess qualities which made him despicable to others. "My 'unusualness,'" he writes, "was gradually beginning to give me the disagreeable, rather uncanny feeling that I must possess repulsive traits, of which I was not aware, that caused my teachers and schoolmates to shun me" (p. 64).

However, Jung developed the psychological resources to counter this tendency to self-hatred. "From the beginning," he remembers,

> I had a sense of destiny, as though my life was assigned to me by fate and had to be fulfilled. This gave me an inner security, and, though I could never prove it to myself, it proved itself to me. *I* did not have this certainty, *it* had me. Nobody could rob me of the conviction that it was enjoined upon me to do what God wanted and not what I wanted. . . . I had the feeling that in all decisive matters I was no longer among men, but was alone with God. (p. 48)

This conviction that he was destined for greatness and thus had to go on living was an effective method of countering the anxiety and despair his family situation engendered.

142

His sister's fate was very different. When she died at the age of fifty-one after undergoing some minor surgery, she was still living with her mother. Johanna Jung had neither a family nor an occupation of her own (p. 112).[35] Perhaps one reason she lived the life of a frail recluse was that, unlike her brother, she did not develop an energizing defense against her parents' pathology.

Jung certainly did achieve a degree of greatness. By pursuing the special destiny he felt was his, he overcame the handicap of having two very troubled parents. He sublimated his feelings about his fears and sufferings into a psychological system which brought him fame and fortune and which continues to attract followers all over the world. But in spite of Jung's own success with his theories, Jungian analysands should realize that the system he championed has deficiencies which, I suggest, originally arose from Jung's reluctance to examine his own family situation.

Because Jungian theory does not look at how early experience contributes to structuring the thoughts and feelings of adulthood, it cannot uncover the roots of much of human behavior. Jung's comment that he was never able to unwind the tangle of his earliest memories should be taken seriously. His childhood memories of the huge phallus, of the shit on the cathedral, of the conflict between personalities number one and number two, remained shrouded in mystery for him. He was driven to mystify these experiences with religious language and ideas. Thus, even though Jung managed to parley his mystifications into the fiscal and emotional currency by which he lived, it is highly questionable whether those of us who need to understand our lives psychologically should try to follow his route.[36]

143

In her book about her own struggle for psychological health, British psychotherapist Nini Herman reflects on the eight years she spent in Jungian analysis. "So in our sessions," writes Herman, "we meandered week by week, through every sort of archetype, 'the Hero,' 'the Wise Old Man,' 'the Virgin Mother' . . . everything except the rages in my heart."[37] Herman is critical of what she calls the Jungian "walkabout," which kept her deepest feelings hidden from view.[38] Even though she credits her Jungian analyst with giving her a degree of internal security simply by continuing their work, she finds "the Zürich school of Jung" very limited because it is "rooted in metaphysics rather than in child psychology."[39] "The Jungian cosmology," she says, "seemed to be above such matters as a baby and her milk."[40] For Herman, Jung's "genius overlooked this fundamental ABC, which it scorned as 'reductive' in its search for higher truths and transcendental nourishment."[41]

I doubt that any metaphysics is ever really so far from such things as "a baby and her milk." Certainly Jung's own metaphysics—his notions of the dark side of God, of the *coniunctio oppositorum,* of the elusive anima, all have a basis in his childhood—a basis we are likely to understand better when more material about Jung's life is made available. The mythic language which Jung used to describe his life had its roots in his history. A close look at Jung looking at himself provides an interesting example of the truth contained in the psychoanalytic postulate that nothing is metaphysical without its first being physical.[42]

After reading earlier versions of this essay, several Jungian therapists have told me that I am very wrong about the kind of Jungian therapy they practice. They assured me they do indeed take careful account of their patients' childhood experiences. Further, they claimed that the instruction Jungian therapists now receive trains practitioners to be very attentive to the personal histories of their patients. I applaud such reforms to the extent they are actually taking place and hope these improvements go much further. However, I am left with a question: If Jungian therapists are realizing that they must become more "Freudian" to be effective healers, why are they still Jungians?

PART THREE

Feminism and Psychoanalysis: Overlaps and Interludes

"The Same Stuff": The Talking Cure of Feminism and Psychoanalysis

In 1970, Shulamith Firestone wrote that "psychoanalysis and feminism are made of the same stuff."[1] Her statement (made in the context of a trenchant critique of psychoanalysis) seemed true to me then. It seems even truer today.

Besides sharing the subject of sexuality (which was the "stuff" of Firestone's comparison), psychoanalysis and feminism have a similar soteriology—a similar way of approaching human salvation. Both analysis and feminism are fundamentally messianic; both are concerned with developing methods and visions of transforming self and world.

An essential salvific method for both psychoanalysis and feminism is human conversation. Both theories construct occasions to encourage a particular kind of talk. Both are interested in talk that first explores and then heals.

In feminism, such talk happens in small gatherings called consciousness-raising groups, support groups, or study groups. Such groups were an essential part of the feminist movement in the early seventies but they persist even now. Feminist organizations continually use the small group technique to confront problems and to renew vitality. One goal of the consciousness-raising session has always been to allow free and honest expression. Since what women have felt and thought has been largely ignored by the dominant cultures for most of recorded history, consciousness-raising sessions give voice to much that has been repressed.

These groups exist to give women a place to say the unsayable. The chance to speak and be heard allows a woman to find new energy to transform a world that has been shutting her up. Even if the transformation never reaches beyond the group, the words exchanged between women can work magic.

My friend, the poet and novelist Joy Kogawa, has written a short story, "Snow White Meets the Mirror on the Wall," using her experience with a group of us who met regularly. In the story, she describes what happens to a fictional Anna, a fifty-year-old woman whose professor husband has just left her to live with a twenty-year-old student. In the following passage, Anna talks to her women friends about her misery over her husband's departure:

> In the name of nothing that afternoon, Anna called her friends—Fernande, Caryll, Marie-Louise, Betty, Debby, Andrea, Naomi, Katherine.
>
> "You're out of it. Thank God you're out of it." She was pummeled by their tears. "Thank God we're not living in Grimm's fairy tales."
>
> "But I am," Anna wailed.
>
> "No you aren't," Naomi said. "This isn't the Dark Ages."
>
> For Anna, however, it still was. And it was in the darkness of the ages that she fought the angel till she was given a new name. She refused both the dream of being Snow White and the dread of being the wicked witch. But she clung to these identities and held them taut till she was given a third option.

And deep down in the middle of the earth, with pickaxe and pail and miner's tiny headlamp, Anna found herself hunting for treasures, for insight and for magic with which to remake her crumpled world. In the depths of the earth, she escaped from the house that envy makes. She practiced her march to love's tiny house hidden in the woods.

In the new morning of her every ordinary day, Anna the Grumpy One, Bashful, Sneezy, Dopey, Hopeful, Sleepy or even Happy Anna, Anna of the seven dwarves rose up and dressed and went down singing to the mines. She returned to the struggle. She put the phone back on the hook. She let the bitterness flow and she let herself weep in her twentieth-century North American dwarfdom.

Then she rewrote the story. She rewrote and rewrote and rewrote the story, late into the morning and into the night, huddling with her sisters in their caves and corners and out on the rooftops. Every wicked witch, old crone and hag in sight was enlisted in the task.

"It isn't easy," they said. "These things take time."

They sat together and sat together in the bowels of the earth—dedicated dwarves meeting to unmake the mirrors that cackle with lies. And with all their might and fire and souls, they melted stones and dragon's gold. They were forging the mirrors that look on the heart.[2]

In Kogawa's story, the only role that Anna can at first see for herself when her husband leaves her is that of an envious hag. Through talk with other women, Anna discovers options. Her personal pain is absorbed by a wider world. By putting her phone back on the hook, Anna, the new kind of hag, puts herself back in touch with the world.

Like the dedicated dwarves in Kogawa's women's group, in a psychoanalytic session, analyst and patient use magic words

151

to forge mirrors that "look on the heart." Although psycho-analysis has established a more formalized structure for talk-ing, the goal of the words spoken is similar to that of con-sciousness-raising groups. In the theater of the analytic session, the unsayable can both be said by the analysand and be listened to by the healer. Pain is transmuted by being brought into a freer association with a range of words, ideas, and experiences. Together, healer and analysand use speech to erode a symptom by bringing it to consciousness and con-necting it to a broader social order.[3]

In *The Journey Is Home,* Nelle Morton remarks on the im-portance of listening a person into speech.[4] Both psychoanaly-sis and feminism create places for this listening to happen. The analytic session and the consciousness-raising group oppose the tendency to make words and texts into fetishes.[5] Both fem-inism and psychoanalysis reveal the human context which pro-duces text. Both encourage people to feel the vitality, the res-onance, and thus the contingency of words. "I had never thought of this," writes Marie Cardinal at the conclusion of her seven-year analysis,

> never understood that any exchange of words was a precious event. It represented a choice. Words were boxes, they con-tained material which was alive. Words could be inoffensive ve-hicles, multicolored bumper cars colliding with one another in ordinary life, causing sparks to spray that did no harm. Words could be vibrating particles, constantly animating existence, or cells swallowing each other like phagocytes or gluttonous corpuscles leaguing together to devour microbes and repulse foreign invasions. Words could be wounds or scars from old wounds, they could resemble a rotten tooth in a smile of pleasure. Words could also be giants, solid boulders going deep down into the earth, thanks to which one can get across

152

the rapids. Words could become monsters, finally, the SS of the unconscious driving back the thought of the living into the prisons of oblivion.[6]

In the local, intimate context of a conversation, psycho-analysis and feminism search for the "thought of the living" that has been imprisoned by a dominant consciousness and a dominant culture. Both deal with liberating what has been repressed for the purpose of incorporating it in a more public world. Both loosen the weave of the social fabric in order to use old strands in a new pattern. Psychoanalysis and feminism both use a talking cure.

Freud says that the goal of psychoanalysis is "Where id was, there ego shall be."[7] This statement, as several analysts have remarked, comes much closer to his German if we drop the Latin and say "where *it* was, there *I* shall be."[8] I suggest that this is not only a central goal for psychoanalysis, but for fem-inism as well. Both are ideologies and procedures which aim to expand the human sense of subjectivity. For both, "where it was, there I shall be" is an ideal before us like a point on the horizon.

Feminism, like every social movement with egalitarian ideals, works to grant public power and recognition to those who have been marginalized. Through feminist efforts, the male voice is no longer the only voice that defines the range of intellectual inquiry. Female voices alter the traditional do-mains of theory, or as some would say, the discourses of mas-tery, and make them more various, more flexible, and more inclusive of human experience.[9] One example of this is Marxist theory, which in feminist hands is expanding to consider "re-productive" labor.[10] Another example is the academic study of religion, which is (slowly) enlarging its focus on theology, the

153

logic of God, to include thealogy, the logic of Goddess.[11] The expansion of the language used by these disciplines broadens and deepens the subjectivity of those who study them. The "egos" of masters and students, their senses of who they are, who they were, and who they can become, grow in range.

Paula Heimann defines "ego" as "the sum-total of an individual's feelings, emotions, impulses, wishes, capacities, talents, thoughts, and phantasies, in short all those psychic forces and formations which a person . . . would identify as his own and which would make him feel: 'That is I.' "[12] Psychoanalysis extends that feeling of "I" by encouraging each analysand to become more familiar with her or his own psychic furnishings. Acceptance of thoughts and emotions or, at least, recognition of them replaces repression, disavowal, and splitting. The personality becomes more flexible and expansive, more able to survive and enjoy a wider world. The free association of thoughts, fantasies, and feelings is what analysis is about. Or, to echo Firestone's words, free association is the "stuff" of psychoanalysis.

Isn't freer association the stuff of feminism too? Doesn't the slogan "the personal is political" call for "a return of the repressed" in order to expand one's sense of immersion in the world? Feminism brings the politics of the unconscious into the public, conscious world by bringing those who have been forced to symbolize the repressed into politics. When the black, feminist, lesbian poet Audre Lorde writes that her purpose is to "act upon you like a drug or a chisel to remind you of your meness, as I discover you in myself," she is promoting a reformation in our political and psychological sense of "I."[13] The same is true of bell hooks, who in *Feminist Theory from Margin to Center* argues for an expansion of the dominant

154

feminist ego beyond exclusive identification with the white middle class.[14]

The feminist plea for extending the communal "I" is not unlike the Freudian plea for extending the psychological "I." One goal does not really happen without the other. The person who feels that a range of identities comprise herself or himself is also likely to be "one" who can feel points of likeness with many who have been labeled "others." The talking cures of both feminism and psychoanalysis amplify the voices of silenced parts of individuals and communities.

T E N

Anger in the Body: The Impact of Idealization on Human Development and Religion

For the past several years, feminist theory from various disciplines has been stressing the inadequacy of the traditional concept of the body in Western thought. A basic feminist argument has been that in order to improve the condition of women and to preserve the environment, we must place greater value on the physical world in general and on human physicality in particular. As Mary Daly writes in *Pure Lust,* we must encourage "biophilia" in our own species.[1]

My goal in this essay is to promote "biophilia" and to take feminist thought about the body a bit further by applying Melanie Klein's theory of aggression to certain religious ideas. I will argue that the suppression of the body in religious traditions is linked to the displacement of aggression in those traditions. Such displacement, I believe, has important consequences for forming notions about deities and for shaping the behavior of groups who identify with those deities. Before setting out these ideas, I will discuss the portions of Klein's theory from which I derive them.[2]

Melanie Klein, whose writings were published in England between 1921 and 1963, was a follower of Freud. Her work focuses psychoanalysis on the experiences of very young children. Because Klein sees a child's early life with the mother as very important, she challenges the Freudian obsession with the father's role in development.

Melanie Klein has been justly criticized for ignoring the influence of cruel or inadequate parental care in causing the rage she witnessed in infants and young children. Nevertheless, although I agree with such criticisms, I see great value in her description of the psychological dynamics involved in the human struggle with anger.

One of the most controversial aspects of Klein's theory is her view that aggression is an innate instinct in every human baby. For many people, Klein's picture of an infant with destructive feelings is even more surprising than Freud's initial picture of an infant with sexual feelings. Consider, for example, Norman O. Brown's concept of infancy as a time of sexual innocence, a time he describes as "protected from the harshness of reality by parental cares . . . a period of privileged irresponsibility . . . which permits and promotes an early blossoming of the essential desires of the human being without repression and under the sign of the pleasure-principle."[3] In Brown's work, the infant is imagined as an untroubled creature delighting in all its bodily functions. In contrast, in Klein's work, infants are seen as beings who are often upset, fearful, and angry.

Klein bases her early ideas about the problems of childhood on close observation of her own three children. She has an advantage over many male theorists, who, we know very well, usually have not had an extensive acquaintance with the details of an infant's life. Perhaps we would have less literature extol-

157

ling the bliss of infancy if the men, such as Brown, who formulated those theories, had been subject to interruptions from babies screaming unblissfully.

Klein believes that coping with anger is a universal problem because every baby experiences frustration and discomfort to some degree. She thinks that angry feelings cause anxiety because anger is felt to be a terrifying internal destructive force which poses a threat from within the body. Klein also believes that children fear retaliation from the things they want to harm.

However, even though she thinks the infant's desires to destroy generate fear of the world, she feels those same desires also inspire interest in the world. Klein believes the child is constantly urged to explore the environment by the need to displace aggressive fantasies. She thinks that if children are extremely reluctant to experience aggression, they are cut off from a necessary channel to the outside world.

In a paper titled "The Importance of Symbol Formation in the Development of the Ego," Klein illustrates her early theoretical formulations by describing her treatment of a four-year-old psychotic boy.[4] The child, whom she calls Dick, can barely talk, seems to have no interest in the outside world, and is largely indifferent to anyone who looks after him. He vacillates between being inappropriately obedient and inappropriately defiant. He has problems urinating and defecating and is often very reluctant to chew any food. The inhibition of biting is what first leads Klein to suspect that Dick was unwilling to express aggressive feelings.

Klein begins Dick's analysis by suggesting that toys in the room represent him and his parents. He then gradually begins to handle the toys in ways that show he feels angry. He sometimes also appears frightened and runs away from his play.

158

Klein applies her technique of child analysis and interprets Dick's actions aloud to him. For example, when he damages a toy cart, she tells him that it is his mother and makes him understand that sometimes he wants to hurt his mother. She finds that such interpretations seem to make Dick feel freer. His range of actions increases and he is more interested in exploring the environment of her consulting room. His aggressive play involves a great number of objects and he starts to talk about what he is doing. Eating and other bodily functions become easier for him.

Klein notices that as Dick's freedom of mind and body increase, so do his expressions of need and affection for her, for his mother, and for the nurse who brings him to the treatment. Like any normal child, he begins to show that he likes those who care for him, that he wants their attention and is upset when they leave him. Thus his new interest in things is paralleled by a willingness to be affected by people.

Klein considers Dick's treatment to be a great success. She believes that his ability to experience aggression is fundamental to both the development of his intellect and to his capacity to feel affection. Her later theories elaborate the ways in which aggression, intellectual freedom, and concern for people are intertwined.

Klein thinks that the most fundamental psychological achievement of childhood is the sustained capacity to feel both love and hate toward the same people and things. This ability is essential for both intellectual and moral development. Her theory posits two psychological stages which culminate in the perception of oneself and other people as complex beings with both good and bad aspects.

The first stage of psychological life predominates in the first three or four months of infancy. It is characterized by the feeling that each event or experience is a separate, concrete thing. The thing, or "object" in Klein's terms, corresponds to the infants' feelings at the moment. For example, the breast or bottle that feeds them is good, but the breast or bottle that frustrates them by its absence is bad. Klein thinks that immature visual perception causes a baby to see the world in fragments. The infants' own bodies and those of the mothers' seem to be just so many disconnected parts.

But in addition to visual immaturity, there is another reason for seeing the world in parts. Klein thinks that babies and young children are afraid that the good, satisfying things in their world may be destroyed by the bad, frustrating things. The baby's sense of well-being, she believes, initially depends on the ability to keep the good and bad objects widely separated. This is the baby's only defense against the fear that the two objects will meet and the good ones will be destroyed. The fear of the annihilation of good things, she thinks, amounts to the fear of death. Thus maintaining experience in good and bad fragments is the earliest method each of us has for coping with this basic terror.

To keep good things far away from things which threaten them, Klein believes that young children split both themselves and other people into good and bad aspects. For example, negative feelings about parents are sometimes projected onto strangers, who then seem terrifying. The strangers represent the fear and anger the child feels toward his or her own parents. The split object of parents/strangers is paralleled, Klein thinks, by a split of love and hate in the child's ego. The frightening parts of both self and world are thus isolated and controlled.

Another way of making sure that aggressive feelings in the first stage of psychological development are kept at bay is for

160

children to exaggerate the goodness of pleasant things and people in their experience. Klein thinks that children tend to idealize parents in order to control their fear of them and anger toward them. Although she thinks that the ability to idealize parents provides important reassurances in childhood, she also thinks it is essentially motivated by a fear of persecution. In order for the world to be seen more realistically, it is necessary for this fear to abate.

In Kleinian theory, what enables the world to come together for children is confidence in the continuing presence of good objects inside their bodies. Klein believes that if children could take in enough love and comfort, they would know that goodness exists inside them and that destruction is not imminent. The growing conviction that goodness resides within allows children to permit aggression to be felt toward good objects. At this point, the second stage of psychological development begins.

In the second stage, psychic reality becomes "increasingly poignant" as children face their own destructive feelings.[5] In Klein's terminology, "persecutory anxiety" now changes to "depressive anxiety." Fear for oneself becomes fear for others. Klein suggests that various inhibitions which small children develop might be techniques to keep depressive anxiety at bay. The refusal to eat, for example, might be an attempt to restrain the wish to bite—an action which, in children's fantasies, might signify a desire to harm people they love.

When self and world are more unified, compassion for people becomes possible. Klein writes that "when . . . destructive impulses and phantasies are felt to be directed against the complete person of a loved object, guilt arises in full strength and, together with it, the over-riding urge to repair, preserve or revive the loved injured object."[6] Klein labels the tendency

161

to cherish and maintain good internal feelings as the desire to make "reparation." She sees all constructive activities in life, all creative work, all caring behavior, as expressions of this urge to aid, nourish, and sustain what she calls "the good object."

I want to stress that, for Klein, the key motive behind the need to care both for people and for work is guilt. Because a person can feel the capacity to destroy life, she or he is continually moved to protect and nourish life. If aggression is not experienced, it will be split off; and thus the motive for concern about the world will be absent. The person will then experience his or her own aggression solely in paranoid form as an alien force threatening the self. This persecutory anxiety will dominate; and the intellect and personality will be restricted along with the capacity to care about other people. Klein says that it is in the second stage that a so-called depressive anxiety spurs the child "to project, deflect and distribute desire and emotion . . . on to new objects and interests."[7] In Klein's thought, it is the guilt and concern which we feel over our desires to destroy our first loved objects which urge us both to explore the world and to cherish it.

I find this a unique picture of human life. In Kleinian theory, we move from a world in pieces to a world tinged with sadness. Klein's own terms are dismal. One moves from the "paranoid-schizoid position" to the "depressive position." Aggression, sadism, or the "death instinct," as Klein sometimes terms it, is always with us. We are forever living with some measure of anxiety and forever keeping it at bay. These are not ideas which are easily accepted.

Nevertheless, I think the time has come to consider the merits of these theories. Klein's work deserves attention precisely because she takes aggression so seriously. We are now living in an epoch in which chemical and nuclear technology have amplified our ability to destroy to frightening levels. In addition, it seems that increasingly violent fantasies are permeating our media and are being consumed by an ever-growing constituency. It is therefore the right moment to consider psychologies such as Klein's that emphasize human aggression. We need to understand our impulses to destroy in order to develop better strategies for curbing them.

Klein tells us that aggression is essential to life. She sees it as an instinct and thus as a source of vitality. If we cannot incorporate aggression, her theory says, we lose interest in the world and we feel inappropriately frightened. We are then moved to split the world and ourselves into idealized all-good parts and despised all-bad parts. It is then that aggression becomes very dangerous.[8]

Klein recommends that aggression be experienced in its proper context, which is love. When human beings can feel the two emotions springing from the same objects and flowing toward the same objects, they lead more balanced lives and, she thinks, more caring lives. In Klein's theory, hate and love both inspire and mediate each other.

Keeping the idea of a context for aggression in mind, I now want to look at some prevalent religious images and ideas. I will argue that some of our basic religious notions have taken aggression out of context and have thus encouraged a hostility to life.

I will begin with the idea that we have "bodies" and "souls." In 1930, Melitta Schmideberg, Klein's daughter, drew attention to how the concept of "soul" functions in religious thought.[9] She suggested that the soul should be understood as an internalized, often idealized, good object. Her paper, "The Role of Psychotic Mechanisms in Cultural Development," focuses on how certain ideas of demons and spirits describe anxiety. "Flight to the object within," writes Schmideberg, is one way of coping with anxiety.[10] The soul becomes an image of internal refuge, the priceless gift of a benevolent parent which functions to balance the fear of the aggressive parent. Schmideberg then observes what we all know so well—"that the soul comes to be regarded as more valuable than the body."[11]

Although she does not give any further interpretation of the soul/body split in religious thought, Schmideberg contributes an invaluable insight into the motive for the contempt of the body in spiritual traditions. The body, I suggest, is where much religious thought consigns human anger. While the soul is seen as pure, valuable, loving, and eternally alive, the body is viewed as tainted, expendable, and the vehicle of death.

This image of the physical, human world as the place of death and imperfection is preserved in modern dualistic psychologies such as Jungian or archetypal psychology. Although these systems of thought try to value the physical world, they fail because the concepts of deathless "archetypes," of a cherished, transhuman "psyche," or of a grandiose "self" become the idealized, split-off portions of people and their world. Such theories usually locate limitation and selfishness in a vilified idea of the ego.[12] The ego is described as being selfish, materialistic, restrictive, and greedy. Therefore, even though the terms change, the Jungian world is still divided into a pure, eternal, and thus "good" part over and against a flawed, mortal, and thus "bad" part. The angry objects, that is, the body, the ego, or the "merely human" are seen as limited and prone to death because they represent the feared portions of the personality, the portions that seem to threaten the person and her or his loved objects with death. The soul, the psyche, or the archetypes are idealizations of the "good" parts of the personality, which are hoped to be forever present and alive.

I suggest that these philosophies which separate the body from the soul are really separating anger and love. If Klein is right, it is the splitting off of human anger from human love that promotes a deadened world and causes hate to search out a scapegoat.

In some Christian traditions, the chief scapegoats of aggression have been the devil in mythology and women in reality. Women are seen as materialistic, tempting, voracious, trivial, and lusty. They supposedly distract men from spiritual contemplation by inspiring sensual longings. Why should sensuality be such a threat to thoughts about God? Perhaps because, as Klein thinks, sensuality stirs up anger.[13] The idealization of God demands that anger be banished to some place far away from God. An all-good God becomes nonsensual and the angry part of such a God is imagined as a very sensual devil. It is no coincidence that Satan is evil *and* sensual. His evil is his anger and depends on his sensuality. The iconography of Satan as a greedy, lusty figure reveals this connection between sensuality and anger.

The ideas which give rise to the mythological image of the devil are not harmless. It is women who become the flesh and blood repositories of the anger the devil depicts. Perhaps women become the "devil's gateway" because everyone who is nurtured by a woman then connects early desire and early rage to the female sex. Indeed, the devil has often been depicted with female breasts. It is this rage which threatens the image of a perfect God. To put it another way, it is this rage which the image of a perfect God is designed to suppress.

I suggest that Christianity finds it impossible to cherish bodies in general and female bodies in particular because the anger felt to reside in the body poses a threat to images of an all-perfect God. Witness, for example, how impossible it has been for Catholicism to tolerate the physical body of Mary. She is supposed to represent the redemption of the physical world by her Assumption up to heaven in her human body. Yet the theological elaboration of Mariology makes Mary's humanity impossible. The doctrines of Jesus's virgin birth and Mary's own immaculate conception deny that Mary had a normal, human, female body. Her physicality is erased further when images of lactation are suppressed beginning in the 1400s.[14] The idealization of Mary demands that she be disembodied because only a disincarnate mother can be loved perfectly. According to Klein, such perfect love requires that someone be hated. Real, physical women provide a "natural" symbol for that hatred.

Protection of deities from fear and anger can be seen in other ways besides the projection of anger onto human physicality. Hostility is often held at bay by more generalized forms of idealization of gods and goddesses. I suggest that extreme idealization, such as insistence on the goodness of God, always masks a physical terror of a parent.

According to Kleinian theory, children fear their parents both because they project their own anger onto them and because they fear retaliation for their destructive wishes. Theorists such as D. W. Winnicott stress the importance of the actual behavior of the parents in encouraging these fantasies. Both Klein and Winnicott maintain that children tend to deny the experience of aggression, and that destructive feelings about the parents must be acknowledged if children are to grow and feel compassion. I suggest that one of the specific ways our religious mythology denies both the aggression of the parent and aggression felt toward the parent is through the notion that parental violence can lead to immortality.

The myth of Demeter and Persephone provides an example. This myth is usually used to illustrate the unselfish love of a mother for her daughter. Any aggression in the story is generally seen as arising from the males in the myth, that is, from Zeus and Hades. Even Philip Slater, whose work generally offers insight into the subject of maternal aggression in Greek myth, writes that "the Demeter-Kore myth . . . is unique in having parental affection as its primary motivational theme."[15] While I do not dispute this, I think some attention should be paid to Demeter's hostility toward children. In the myth, Demeter takes the baby for whom she is caring as a nurse and dips him repeatedly in the fire. The myth rationalizes the action by explaining it as a rite to make the baby immortal. But we should be suspicious of the explanation. The child's mortal mother is horrified at finding her son in the flames: "the strange woman buries you deep in fire and works grief and bitter sorrow for me," she says.[16] Perhaps the mortal mother understands the murderous intent of the rite correctly. The mortal mother and the divine mother may well represent a split image of one mother who has the capacity both to harm and to save her child.

It is interesting that directly after the fire ritual is interrupted, Demeter, in her anger, threatens to starve the whole human race. When this threat of starvation is placed alongside the story of the child in the fire, a powerful image of maternal rage emerges. I suggest that Demeter's concern about Persephone not blind us to her hostility to other children in the myth. Perhaps the image of the child is also split between the one she cherishes, Persephone, and the ones she threatens, Demophoön, the baby in the fire, and the whole human race.

Once we see Demeter in a less idealized manner, we notice some interesting things about Hades. In the myth, it is Hades who feeds Persephone. He replaces the earth mother as the parent who feeds and by doing so wins the right to have Persephone with him for half of the year. (In this interpretation, I am treating Hades and Zeus as a combined image of father and lover.) Remember, the story begins with Persephone playing "apart from Demeter."[17] The myth places the estrangement from the mother in a causal relation to the attraction to the father as a source of nurture. Of course, the attraction also is a seduction; the food, consisting of those six famous pomegranate seeds, is associated with semen. Nevertheless, the fantasy of receiving food from the father is present amid all the imagery of rape.

Perhaps Persephone turns to the father because she senses that Demeter could be an unreliable provider of food. Klein believes that at the time of weaning a child often turns away from the mother in anger and sees the father as the preferred parent. She thinks that the child then imagines the penis of the father as a perfect breast. After a short time, however, the child becomes disappointed with the father's capacity to nurture and returns to the mother once again. But once the initial estrangement from the mother occurs, early childhood is lived in alternate phases of preferring each parent in turn. This theory can, perhaps, shed some light on why Persephone must shuttle between mother and father after she swallows the seeds.

The myth may well illustrate the vacillation between the different kinds of love and fear which a daughter has for both parents. The mother is feared and hated when she doesn't give food. Winter (when Demeter and Persephone are separated) then comes to be imagined as the mother's angry absence. Likewise, the father is feared and hated for his seductiveness. A desire to be fed by him is then seen as synonymous with wanting sex with him and incurring the mother's anger.

168

It may well be that the wish to maintain unambivalent feelings toward one parent has caused interpreters to overlook some of Demeter's imperfections and to leave out the importance of the feeding Hades does. I do not think much real harm is done by this idealized interpretation of a classical myth. However, in the Christ story, we can see that interpreters' eagerness to excuse the hostility of a deity may have had and still has serious consequences.

Christ himself seems to have been aware of both his own fear of his father and of his father's malice toward him. Carl Jung, in *Answer to Job*, asks why Christ would beseech God "not to lead us into temptation" if he did not fear the malicious side of the Almighty.[18] It is clear to Jung that Jesus feels his father's complicity in his crucifixion because on the cross he cries, "My God, my God why hast thou forsaken me?"[19]

The Resurrection may well function as a denial of God's violence to his son. Christian theologians throughout the ages have largely ignored negative aspects of the divine parent-child relationship. Their refusal to recognize hostility within the parental image of God has encouraged some devotees of the Christian God to blame Christ's murder on a group of outsiders, the Jews. By identifying themselves with an idealized concept of God, Christians have at certain points in history avoided recognizing their own malice.[20]

Sustained reflection on the tendency to project aggression outward is extremely difficult for any person or group. Nevertheless, such reflection may lead to the discovery of ideas and institutions with both a greater vitality and a greater potential for encouraging empathy and concern. In 1933, in a paper titled "The Early Development of Conscience in the Child," Klein wrote that,

169

the repeated attempts that have been made to improve humanity—in particular to make it more peaceable—have failed, because nobody has understood the full depth and vigor of the instincts of aggression innate in each individual. Such efforts do not seek to do more than encourage the positive, well-wishing impulses of the person while denying or suppressing his aggressive ones. And so they have been doomed to failure from the beginning.[21]

In contrast to many other "repeated attempts to improve humanity," I think feminist theory has a chance for more success. Feminists may well give birth to ways of thinking that promote compassion because we must explain hatred of the body. Feminists must study loathing of the flesh wherever it occurs—whether in individuals, in culture, or in philosophical and religious thought. This direction of research is primary for our inquiry because women represent the body in human culture. We cannot learn to stop hating women without learning to stop hating human flesh.

Klein's work suggests that denigration of the body can only be explained by a profound understanding of the centrality of aggression in human life. I think that feminists should recognize, as she does, that all humans are beings whose destructiveness is as basic as their love. However, we must also go beyond Klein. We must begin to examine the effects that abuse and deprivation have on the engendering of human rage.

Klein also does not extensively describe how the aggression of men differs from that of women. Perhaps male aggression is more destructive because it is for some reason more split off from contexts of affection. In contrast to women, men lead more compartmentalized lives in which they keep hatred and love separate. Carol Gilligan's work shows how women tend to experience a universe of complex feelings when they make

170

moral choices. Men, however, simplify decisions by depending on rules.[22] One consequence of men's estrangement from the turbulence of emotions may be that their aggression is less tempered than that of women. The invention of machines to commit murder is perhaps a dangerous result of the male ability to disembody and decontextualize anger. Their hatred is less mediated by the ambivalence of sympathy.

Any future inquiry into the differences between the aggressiveness of men and that of women must avoid the common feminist propensity to idealize women. For a long time, an important part of feminist ideology has been the relative innocence of women in comparison with men. As so many fine theorists argue, because women have not been the direct architects of violent institutions, they are more likely to dismantle those institutions. I agree. However, if we women are to be successful at creating more humane social institutions, we must not become too enamored with a rhetoric of female purity.

Feminist groups are often torn apart by bitter internal battles which arise from powerful hostilities. Frequently, these hostilities are insufficiently analyzed by the women involved. When such destructiveness is left to fester, it can erupt again and interfere with the agenda of other feminist alliances. I suggest that the women's movement needs to use more thoughtful approaches, such as those offered by psychoanalytic theory, to explore the dynamics of aggression among women. We need to be more willing to acknowledge both the grand and the petty ambitions and animosities which fuel so much of our human energies. As is true of all associations, sisterhoods which are able both to endure and to foster progress in human community-building cannot be founded on an idealized estimation of the goodness of their members.

ELEVEN

The Body of Knowledge: Religious Notions in the Convergence of Psychoanalysis and Feminism

We have been progressively dehumanizing ourselves by taking our human senses, human functions, human parts and abstracting them from our human bodies. We then create machines to do our seeing, listening, touching, talking, or thinking for us in a more perfect form. I see nothing wrong with this when we use machines to support and enhance life—as in the case of artificial limbs or with the use of labor-saving technology. The problem arises when we begin to envy the machines—when we try to imitate them and thus model ourselves on inanimate objects. We then lose touch with what it is to be human.

But it isn't just with machines that we dissociate ourselves from our humanness. I think there are certain habits deep in Western thought that we must examine. There are customary ways of thinking that encourage us to flee from what is human and to despise ourselves. I think that we fall into these habits—these flights from people—whenever we imagine ourselves in any fashion as controlled or influenced by purposeful entities outside ourselves. Religions usually call these things gods; in philosophy, Plato calls them forms; and in psychology, Jung calls them archetypes. By treating these things as real, we distort our world and dehumanize ourselves.

I think that we need to shrink from theories that foster contempt for physical life. At present, our human race is threatening the entire world with both nuclear holocaust and chemical pollution. We have become a species which spends approximately half of our collective energy and resources in devising our own destruction. I am not at all sure that intellectual practice can do much to assuage such danger. But we have to try. We must immerse ourselves in theories that support life.

I suggest that many of our Western religious traditions can now offer little help in formulating strategies for living. The concept of a God who is outside the context of human contingency is itself a machine fantasy. *Deus est machina.* By imagining any rules or laws, any propensity toward good or evil, any knowledge or wisdom, as coming from outside a human sphere, we fuel the modern contempt for what is human. A transcendent godhead is an idea we can no longer afford.

But what then? What sort of theory can now carry a salvific message? I suggest that such theory lies in a place theology has shunned—the human body. Instead of theology, I recommend two bodies of theory that appreciate human physicality: psychoanalysis and feminism.

Theology versus Psychoanalysis

The idea of finding grounds for an optimistic view of human possibility within the corpus of psychoanalytic theory is ridiculous from the standpoint of traditional theology. It is generally concluded among theologians who discuss Freud that if one stays with the psychoanalytic perspective the world looks

173

quite bleak and life is emptied of hope. This was the opinion of Oskar Pfister, a contemporary of Freud, who called his critique of Freud's *Future of an Illusion,* the *Illusion of a Future.* More recently, Hans Küng has expressed the hopelessness he sees in accepting Freudianism. "Religious belief," Küng writes,

> would be in a bad way if there were no genuine grounds for it or if no grounds remained after a psychoanalytic treatment of the subject; however devout its appearance, such a faith would be immature, infantile, perhaps even neurotic. . . . Why should I not be allowed to wish that the sweat, blood, and tears, all the sufferings of millennia, may not have been in vain, that definitive happiness may finally be possible for all human beings— especially the despised and the downtrodden? And why should I not, on the other hand, feel an aversion to being required to be satisfied with rare moments of happiness and—for the rest—to come to terms with "normal unhappiness"? . . . May I not feel an aversion also in regard to the idea that the life of the individual and of mankind is governed only by the pitiless laws of nature, by the play of chance, and by the survival of the fittest, and that all dying is a dying into nothingness?[1]

Note how insufficient and unsatisfying Küng finds the physical world. Because this world appears dismal and harsh, another world becomes necessary—a world of God, which he sees as "the Unconditioned."[2] For Küng, this "unconditioned" reality that is "independent of our thinking, willing and feeling, of psyche and society," is where hope resides.[3]

The work of Paul Ricoeur strikes a similar theme. Although Ricoeur greatly admires Freud, he is ultimately dissatisfied with the materialism of psychoanalytic theory. "In our day," he writes, "reductive hermeneutics is no longer a private affair; it has become a public process, a cultural phenomenon;

whether we call it demythologization, when it occurs in a given religion, or demystification, when it proceeds from without, the aim is the same: the death of the metaphysical and religious object. Freudianism is one of the roads to this death."[4]

Ricoeur wants to use Freudian theory in the work of restoring a more authentic faith. Psychoanalysis, he thinks, can help us see through the idolatry clinging to religious symbols in culture. It can then lead us to glimpse something he calls the "Wholly Other"—which he contrasts to "the human world of culture."[5] Thus, for Ricoeur just as for Küng, that which is truly meaningful is positioned outside of the physical, human universe with which psychoanalysis is concerned.

The same uneasiness with the Freudian perspective can also be glimpsed in the work of Peter Homans. I say "glimpsed" because Homans is always very careful not to side with psychoanalysis or religion. Yet in *Theology after Freud*, he refers to "the grim and comfortless conclusion of Freud's 'analytic' of religion, his 'antitheology.'"[6] Homans proposes no easy answer to the grimness he sees in Freud. He suggests that theorists maintain "an active, real tension in which identification with Freud and aloof, rebellious, active dismissal of his theories are avoided."[7]

Homans might well be right. Perhaps it is inappropriate to abandon the pretense of a neutral perspective on the dispute between psychoanalysis and religion and to advocate one view over another. But this is the folly in which I am engaged.

I suggest that the conflict between psychoanalysis and religion can be usefully seen as a conflict about the body and what the body knows. Religion, on the one hand, sees the source of some kinds of knowledge—namely, "religious" knowledge—as lying outside the body. It maintains that there is a purposeful reality external to human beings which can affect, direct, or instruct human existence. Psychoanalysis, on the other hand, refuses to accept an external source for any human knowledge. Psychoanalysis sees human knowledge as growing out of wholly human experience. For psychoanalysis, the word "knowledge" is similar to the word "thought" or "idea." All knowledge, all thought, all ideas come from somatic sources. To put it very simply, and I think, not too simply, in psychoanalysis all knowledge is carnal knowledge.

Now what if we hold the analytic view to be true and take the Freudian and post-Freudian perspectives very seriously? What if we abandon all dogma about transcendence and resolve to stay with psychoanalysis in its relentless insistence on the physical nature of human beings and human knowledge? Do we, as theologians maintain, wind up in a bleak, grim physical world? Just how hopeless is the body?

"Body" in Religion and Psychoanalysis

Body certainly is hopeless if we conceive it in terms of the major traditions of Western philosophy. The dominant theme in Western thought since Plato has been that the body is a vehicle for a higher entity—mind or soul. The body is thought of as being a temporary place where mind, soul, or psyche resides. General knowledge, it is believed, develops in the mind. Religious knowledge, however, is thought of as emanating from something even higher than mind or soul. Various terms—gods, forms, archetypes—are used to refer to the thing outside of mind, the thing which informs the mind.

I am simplifying the differences among these terms in order to point out a basic difference between a religious notion of the person and a psychoanalytic one. There is always a duality

176

about the human being in religions such as Christianity, Islam, and Judaism; in philosophies that are religious, such as Platonism; and in psychologies that are religious, such as Jungian psychology.[8] Something—usually mind or soul—is contrasted with body, and is then seen as better, nobler, cleaner, and ultimately of a different character or substance than the body. In such religious views of the person, the higher part is seen as being closer to whatever is accorded divine, directive status. The soul is closer to the forms. The psyche is linked with the archetypes. And mind or reason is joined with God.

If we accept this familiar dualistic view of the person, the body becomes unimportant. This happens because all the truly fine things about human beings are seen as coming from the mind or soul, which in turn is believed to have obtained the good things from something wholly transcendent to anything physical. I would argue that this view of the person as having two parts, one of which is "better" in the sense of being closer to God, holds true in general terms for both Christianity and Judaism. In both religions, the flesh is seen as needing salvation. In Christianity, the flesh is redeemed by Jesus' sacrifice; in Judaism, it is saved by adherence to God's rules for living. In both religions, the body is slighted because something other than body—indeed, something other than human—is placed in charge. The body then becomes dumb. It can only be "mere" body—the "apparatus for life," as D. H. Lawrence once said.[9]

In contrast to this religious conception of body, there is the psychoanalytic view. In psychoanalysis, the body becomes more complex because the mind is never separated from it. All of the fine things about human beings—their intellects, their morality, their aesthetic sensibilities—arise from bodily sources. Many have seen this analytic view as reductive be-

177

cause mind and soul are reduced to body. I would put it another way. Instead of reducing the mind, psychoanalysis elevates the body by granting it all the qualities which most of Western philosophy reserves for the mind.

The respect of psychoanalysis for the complexity of body lies in its origins as a mode of treatment for the bodily ailments of women in the nineteenth century. Josef Breuer and Sigmund Freud used their "talking cure" as a way of interpreting and influencing the human body. "Hysterics," Freud writes, "suffer mainly from reminiscences."[10] It is the conversation between doctor and patient which touches these reminiscences and thus eases bodily sufferings. According to early analytic theory, hysterics translate or "convert" their memories into physical agonies. They write their sufferings in flesh. By bringing the memories to conscious attention, Freud believes that their power can be worn away.[11] Some feminist scholars describe early analytic therapy as a technique for interpreting the body language of women.[12]

No matter how complex Freud's later theory became, it never lost this original focus. It never departed from the notion that the flesh is cognizant of its history. In his later works, Freud expressed the hope that scientific progress would one day enable psychoanalysis to formulate psychological statements in physiological terms. "We must recollect," he said in 1914, "that all our provisional ideas in psychology will presumably some day be based on an organic substructure."[13] Later, in 1939, he explained that psychoanalysis identifies "what is truly psychical" with somatic phenomena. The concept of the unconscious, he suggested, is how analysis refers to somatic processes which future research might name more precisely.[14]

178

The early discovery that memory resides in the body means that, in psychoanalysis, every physical experience is metaphoric. For example, in psychoanalysis, sex can never be a simple activity of the genitals. Instead, analysis sees sex as involved with earlier experiences of nutrition, excretion, muscular excitation, and sensory activity. Genital sexuality, just as other physical experiences, reverberates with echoes of childhood and infancy. For psychoanalysis, the flesh can never be literal since, as long as it lives, it teems with past memories and wishes for the future. Body is forever imaging its desires and forever elaborating its past.

Thus, in a Freudian perspective, the body becomes the complex context of all experience. The body is seen as charged with an intellect or, more accurately, with an energy that is constantly expressing somatic history. Thought is one form of this expression; action is another. For psychoanalysis, thought, like action, is itself an activity of the body. It is this notion of body as the matrix of human cognition that, I suggest, must animate modern philosophy, if that philosophy is to foster respect for life.

Thoughts, Words, and Physical History

The relationship between thought as expressed in words and bodily life is necessarily stressed in psychoanalysis since treatment aims to alter physical conditions via language. British psychoanalyst Charles Rycroft writes: "It is the fact that words can symbolize instinctive acts and objects and carry cathexes derived from them that makes psychoanalytical treatment possible."[15] For analysis, then, mental phenomena such as words, thoughts, or ideas are never disembodied. Rather, they are

179

conditioned both by somatic drives and by the past physical and social context in which those drives were experienced.

Freud believes that for thought to be healthy, it must always connect with the experiential context from which it arises. For example, he describes schizophrenia as a condition in which the link between words and what they represent is severed. "When we think in abstractions," he writes, "there is a danger that we may neglect the relations of words to unconscious thing-presentations, and it must be confessed that the expression and content of our philosophizing then begins to acquire an unwelcome resemblance to the mode of operation of schizophrenics."[16] This stress on seeking the origin of thought in past somatic experience explains Freud's attitude toward words as phenomena which lead backwards and which carry meaning because they are conditioned by memories, by sense perceptions, and by bodily history.

I find it significant that Paul Ricoeur, who tries very hard to make Freudian psychoanalysis compatible with a spiritual view of humankind, finds Freud's ideas of linguistic meaning insupportable. "Unfortunately," says Ricoeur, "the Freudian conception of language is very inadequate, [namely, that] the meaning of words is the revival of acoustic images; thus language itself is a 'trace' of perception. This vestigial conception of language can give no support to an epigenesis of meaning."[17] Ricoeur's discomfort with Freud's view of language as a condensation of various sense perceptions is important because it is a basic criticism of how analysis searches for meaning.

Ricoeur sees the psychoanalytic activity of connecting words to past feelings, past sensations, and past impressions as incapable of providing a meaning for the future—a meaning that is "higher." He is right about this. Analysis can support no "epigenesis" of meaning when that meaning is seen as lying beyond or outside the body and the textured intimacy of its past. Ricoeur's desire for a meaning to supplement psychoanalytic method is a desire for transcendence. It is a form of the wish for an escape from the conditioning of body.

Motives for and Consequences of the Separation of Mind and Body

It is not enough for me to criticize such wishes for transcendence. Even if I am correct that philosophies advocating transcendence have contributed to our present contempt for physical life, criticism alone will not lead to change. There is also a need to understand why disembodied theory has evolved at all. Why is the transcendence of mind so attractive? There are some interesting approaches to an answer in post-Freudian analytic thought. These theories are useful in uncovering possible motives behind philosophical systems which strive for distance from human flesh and social context.

Freud realizes that the separation of mind and body is a fact of human experience. In *The Question of Lay Analysis*, he writes: "However much philosophy may ignore the gulf between the physical and the mental, it still exists for our immediate experience and still more for our practical endeavors."[18] In a letter to Oskar Pfister in 1930, he says the same thing in a more personal way:

> You are right in saying that my mental powers have not dwindled with my surplus years (over seventy). Though they show the influence of age plainly enough. There are three ways of disintegration between which nature takes her choice in individual cases—simultaneous destruction of mind and body, premature mental decay accompanied by physical preservation,

survival of mental life accompanied by physical decrepitude; and in my case it is the third and most merciful of these which has set in.[19]

From such statements, we see that Freud considers the mind's tendency to feel separate from the body as common-sense reality. Further, it is clear that he recognizes this feeling of separateness as a blessing in age and infirmity. But he doesn't develop these ideas any further. It is left to later theorists to explore why the mind distances itself from body and to speculate on how this tendency becomes pathological.

Ernest Jones begins the theorizing with his statements questioning whether mind exists at all. "Speaking for myself only," Jones says, "I will say freely that I know of no reason for believing that mental phenomena can occur anywhere apart from bodily ones, and furthermore I see no reason to believe that such an entity as mind exists at all, whether attached to the body or not."[20] Elsewhere, he phrases it this way,

> I venture to predict that . . . the antithesis [between mind and body] which has baffled all the philosophers will be found to be based on an illusion. . . . When we talk of the mind influencing the body or the body influencing the mind we are merely using a convenient shorthand for a more cumbrous phrase.[21]

Jones's invitation to explore mind's illusion that it is separate from the body is taken up by D. W. Winnicott in his essay titled "Mind and Its Relation to the Psyche-Soma."[22] All our thoughts, our images, our dreams, our emotions—in other words, the "psyche"—are, according to Winnicott, elaborations of body, or to use his terms, of "physical aliveness." Ideally, Winnicott feels, the psyche should be felt to animate the entire organism. This notion of psyche does, I think, capture the pervasive "alive" qualities imputed to soul in mystical literature. However, it has the advantage of being precise and more somatic.

A consequence of the estrangement of what we have called mind from what we have called body might well be the suppression of affective, emotional content in much of scientific and philosophic tradition. Charles Rycroft refers to "the pathology of the Western intellectual tradition" as being "the dissociation of wishful, fantasy thought, from adaptive 'objective' thought."[23] In an essay called "Beyond the Reality Principle," Rycroft suggests that fantasy underlies any healthy person's sense of reality.[24] He hypothesizes that for the adequately mothered infant, wish and reality will not be felt to be too disparate. In such cases, what the body wants and wishes for will generally be what appears. Objective reality will then be experienced as coinciding with the internal bodily world of wishes—wishes for food, for warmth, for physical affection. Rycroft believes that classical analytic theory has been too ready to separate wishful or "primary process" thinking from adaptive or "secondary process" thinking. This attitude, he says, comes from the modern scientific prejudice in which humankind is supposed to view the world "from two unconnected and incompatible standpoints, one scientific and objective, the other imaginative and subjective."[25]

Although he thinks that Western scientific rationalism has made some good use of the capacity of human thought to strive for objectivity—that is, to try to view the world "without interference from emotional bias and animistic thinking"[26]—Rycroft wonders whether the dissociation has become compulsive. When we suppress the emotional, wishful facets of our human rationality, our lives lose their luster and our reason is severed from sources of "spontaneous life."[27] That spontaneous life, that wishful, emotional desire for the world, arises from our bodies. Thus the trick to maintaining the sparkle is within the body. It lies, according to Rycroft, in never forgetting that "spiritual or cultural functions are equally and simultaneously biological functions."[28] It lies, in Adrienne Rich's words, in never forgetting that "all our high-toned questions breed in a lively animal."[29]

Since psychoanalysis does not consider thought as separate from its emotional and social context, it can encourage investigation of the affective basis of our theorizing. Awareness of this analytic perspective can, perhaps, discourage the tradition of building massive theoretical systems on the illusion of a disembodied intellect. Philosophy can thus perhaps be prodded into greater involvement with life.

By itself, however, I do not think that psychoanalysis has much possibility of directing Western thought toward a large-scale appreciation of human physicality. Psychoanalysis has too small an audience and is too esoteric to influence cultural life very much.

Feminism, Psychoanalysis, and the Body

The movement which has a greater chance of bringing Western thought back to the body is feminism. Feminism can pervade society more than can psychoanalysis. The women's movement can reach beyond therapeutic consulting rooms and academic journals into the fabric of daily life. Although psychoanalysis can become part of feminism and thus share its impact, it has little chance of having significant influence on its own.

As I have said before, feminism can become a vehicle for psychoanalytic insight because psychoanalysis and feminism

184

share the theme of sexuality.[30] Feminists uncover issues relating to sexuality and physicality in respected philosophical, moral, and religious systems, just as Freudians reveal physical and emotional motives behind the rational structures of culture. Both theories continually remind us of the bodily ideas concealed in the products and behavior of "higher" civilization.

Both psychoanalytic theory and feminist theory lead back to the body through their insistence on the importance and complexity of sexuality. Certainly, there are important differences between the two outlooks. Psychoanalysis predates feminism and has so far failed to examine itself in the light of feminist argument. Reading Freud and many other psychoanalytic thinkers from a feminist perspective is as disturbing as it is revealing. Psychoanalytic literature is rife with male bias: bias toward male anatomy, traditional male roles, and ubiquitous male privilege. Sometimes Freud's sexism is merely funny, such as his warning to Wilhelm Fliess to keep the early drafts about the sexual etiology of the neuroses away from Fliess's "young wife."[31] But sometimes, Freud's sexism is maddening, such as his insistence on the moral inferiority of women.[32] These sexist origins make it imperative for psychoanalysis to reconsider its appraisal of the female body and, concomitantly, to reevaluate its view of the female psyche.

By combining the perspectives of feminism and psychoanalysis on the topic of sexuality, gaps in the outlooks of both can be filled in. It is well-known, especially among the British psychoanalysts, that Freud fails to observe and appreciate the importance of infancy and very early childhood in structuring personality and character. This pre-Oedipal period is, of course, the time when women generally dominate a young child's world. The work of Melanie Klein focuses psychoana-

185

lytic theory on this phase of human development.[33] Klein, the mother of three children, was not a feminist. Nevertheless, her work brings a woman's perspective to psychoanalysis.[34] Male theorists such as W. R. Bion and D. W. Winnicott were influenced by Klein, and in part as a result of her work, analytic thinking in Britain started to focus on babies and women's role as mothers.

Although Kleinian theory does not do justice to women in roles other than that of mother, at least it begins to look at the importance of women in shaping civilization. Klein points out that each sex becomes aware of itself in relation to a *woman's* body. The first experiences of flesh, and, if Klein is right, the most formative experiences of flesh, take place exclusively within a female physical context. Thus our first subject of study—our first body of knowledge—is a female body. It is no wonder that in Greek mythology, the nine Muses, who inspire all the arts and sciences, are pictured as female. In a Kleinian view, all efforts to know anything have their origins in the initial human project of knowing the mother's body as the source of all nutrition and all comfort. The physical interplay of mother and child forms the matrix of all knowing. Thus Klein's ideas shed light on why women generally represent the body in so much of Western philosophy and iconography.

The deep psychic association of women with body could bring the consciousness of body to much scholarship in the decades ahead, if feminist theory becomes more a part of academic disciplines. In a sense, attending to women's writing is listening to the body talk. What will the body say that is new?[35] It is most likely that women will actually write things that are very old. One of the most valuable contributions feminism can make to discourse is that of fostering writing and speaking styles that reveal their subjective origins in the personal and collective past. Feminist writing at its best, I think, can shatter the illusion of objectivity which turns so much modern scholarship into mechanized jargon. It can return rationality to its roots in emotion and body.

I visualize this goal for feminism through an image from Greek history. At certain times in the long history of the Delphic oracle, the female priestess known as the Pythia would prophesize in ecstatic gibberish. A male priest would then interpret her utterances and give the petitioner the oracle's reply. It was the priest's job to make sense of the priestess's babble.

This relationship between pythia and priest typifies the stereotyped roles played by men and women throughout much of history. Women play the role of the fecund yet inarticulate body—full of magic and mysterious wisdom. Men, in contrast, play the role of the "Word"—full of meaning and objective definitions. One could say that women, forced to play the pythias of civilization, have spoken in the language of primary process—immediate, emotional, and physical. Men, in contrast, have spoken in the language of secondary process with a style more distant, cool, and detached. It occurs to me that the role of the Pythia was played by all the female hysterics whose ramblings and bodily postures were then interpreted by Freud and Breuer, who became the high priests of psychoanalysis. Analysis itself thus became an activity which interprets primary process thinking in terms of secondary process language. Its power derives from a melding of gender-specific modes of expression.

The widespread illusion that primary and secondary process thought are separate—or, to put it another way, the perception that fantasy is separate from objective thought—is sus-

187

tained by the separation of men and women into rigid roles such as priest and pythia. Women are seen as the inarticulate body because women form the human universe when babbling is the only human speech possible. The gibberish of primary process and the overwhelming physical desires of infancy are, at present, almost exclusively linked with women. When men share in the care of infants, the symbols of this early time will change. It will be possible to imagine men as body as well.

It is even just possible that shared childcare will not be necessary to alter our imagination. The symbolism of body and mind might well change from the direction of adulthood as women become more articulate, more obvious in every aspect of public culture.

In any case, the possibility of imagining body as male is not the most significant change that feminism could effect. As women speak more and are heard more in public settings, the human body could become increasingly coherent and increasingly influential. It could become more difficult to advocate philosophical systems in which words are far abstracted from their relationships to the somatic world. Hermeneutics might then discover the original text, that is, the human body. In the beginning was definitely not the Word. The biblical statement reverses the order. It is flesh that makes the words.

A new hermeneutics will have to recognize the perpetual subversion of the body. All our systems of thought, all our disciplines of knowledge, are perpetually, continually changing and thus perpetually and continually inaccurate. Our systems can only be approximations of our always desiring, always alive, very human bodies. Thus, paradoxically, when our systems become more approximate, and less sacred, they become truer and closer to life.

Because our bodies never cease echoing the past in new ways, with new variations, there is always more to say and always more to want. The body cannot be literal as long as it is alive, and thus it can never be contained in philosophies that lack contact with somatic imagination. Disembodied theories cannot really describe life; they can only encourage us to limit it.

For all my talk against traditional religion, I have actually preached quite a bit. This could be a warning that the philosophy I am advocating could be as full of pious rhetoric as any religion. I think this is probably impossible to avoid. I only hope that a feminist rhetoric based in the body inspires theories that value life more than has a patriarchal rhetoric based in the mind.

The Return of the Goddess: Psychoanalytic Reflections on the Shift from Theology to Thealogy

I borrowed the title "The Return of the Goddess" from a series of radio documentaries about feminism and religion produced by the Canadian Broadcasting Corporation.[1] The title describes the direction of much of the work being done by the scholars, artists, and religious leaders who are making a new place for women in contemporary religious thought. Some of the women who are doing this often call themselves witches or members of the sisterhood of the Wicca. They are engaged in founding alternative religions which place the Goddess at the center of worship.[2] Others are working within traditional religious denominations to champion the use of female symbols to refer to God.[3] Still others are interested in finding and elaborating female images of divinities within the fields of psychology, literature, art, and history.[4] Instead of naming themselves "witches," these last two groups identify in a more general way with what is usually called the women's spirituality movement. The efforts of all such women are making the return of the Goddess a definite cultural event—an event which religious leaders, theologians, and scholars of religion are beginning to notice.

Eventually, theology and each disciplinary specialty within religious studies—history of religion, sociology of religion, philosophy of religion, and psychology of religion—will have to face "the Goddess" and to encounter the "thealogy" that reflection on her is creating.[5] This essay is my effort to approach thealogy as a feminist scholar of the psychology of religion. I want to begin to assess the impact of the Goddess movement from the perspective of psychoanalytic theory.

In addition to explaining how analytic thought can be used to understand the Goddess, I also intend to show how the Goddess movement can illuminate certain trends within psychoanalysis. To accomplish this dual purpose, I will concentrate first on four tendencies that I see as common to both ways of thinking. I suggest that anyone who thinks in the terms of either contemporary psychoanalytic theory or of the Goddess movement is urged (1) to focus on the past as a central source of meaning; (2) to focus on female images of power and desire and therefore to deconstruct central images of patriarchal authority; (3) to describe the individual as formed within the context of a community; and (4) to recognize fantasy as a key structure of "rational" thought.

These basic similarities between psychoanalytic theory and avant-garde religious feminism seem to point to an even larger movement in Western thought—a movement which, I think, turns the traditional Platonic world view inside out. I will discuss how both modern analytic theory and ancient Goddess mythology present the same alternative to Plato after I explain

191

my reasons for considering these two ways of thinking as very much alike.

The branch of psychoanalytic theory which is most relevant to feminist thealogy is object relations theory. This highly influential offshoot of earlier Freudian theory developed in Britain out of the work of analysts such as Melanie Klein, W. R. D. Fairbairn, D. W. Winnicott, and Michael Balint.[6] Object relations theory is usually contrasted to the classical approach to psychoanalysis, which is often termed "instinct theory" or "drive theory." Instinct theory depicts the person as an individual, a separate being who is motivated by the vicissitudes of certain basic "drives" which are believed to be inherent in the human organism. In contrast, object relations theory stresses the interconnectedness of people. To an object relations analyst, a person is always seeking relationships with "objects"—that is, with people—with whom a shared world of feelings and activities can be constructed. In general, then, object relations theory focuses more on the human being in relationship to others, while instinct theory is more concerned with the psychodynamics of human subjects thought of as more or less discrete entities.[7]

Another difference between the approach of object relations and that of instinct theory, is that object relations tends to reach further back into childhood. Classical Freudian analysis had been chiefly interested in the human being after the age of five. In contrast, object relations theory began to stress the developmental significance of infancy and very early childhood. Contemporary object relations theorists conceptualize nearly every aspect of a person's behavior and character against the background of the earliest beginnings of her or his life.

Looking to the Past in both Goddess Religion and Psychoanalysis

Object relations theory's intense interest in the deep past is, in broad terms, quite similar to that of the contemporary Goddess religions. Both psychoanalysis and the new thealogies involve participants in an extensive reflection on what happened long, long ago. In psychoanalysis, an individual's preverbal past is judged to be most important. In Goddess religion, emphasis is placed on the collective prehistoric past.

For both philosophies, a sense of connection to the past is cultivated for the purpose of heightening involvement in the present. In the case of Goddess religion, this focus on the past is used to confer a sense of reality and legitimacy on contemporary women's experience. Books about Goddess mythology provide women with a compendium of female passions and sensibilities. The myths are used to call attention to the complexity of female experience and to dignify that experience by revealing its ancient roots. Thus, to a large degree, Goddess religion pursues meaning in the way that Mircea Eliade describes in his work on myths of "eternal return," which confer meaning on the present by recalling ancient stories related to the foundation of culture.[8]

In addition to using stories and images of goddesses to acquaint women with the deep background of their psychological lives, the Goddess movement relates the present to the past through its use of rituals marking the progression of time. Observing major and minor sabbaths tied to the four seasons and to the two solstices and equinoxes keeps alive a sense of connection to nature's recurring pattern of change. Similarly, attention to the phases of the moon links daily life to a

193

monthly cycle of repetition. Present time is thus given weight and significance by explicitly linking it to seasonal and astrological timelessness.

It is probably correct to say that psychoanalysis, particularly as it has been elaborated by object relations theorists, places an even greater value on the redemptive value of connection to the past than does Goddess religion. All analytic theory aims at learning to see more about the past in the psychological structures of the present. No event is ever seen as determined wholly by present circumstance or by motives for a future end. In analysis, the present is largely a *fiction* of the past. The present is a formation or a construction of the past in the sense of the Latin root of the word "fiction" (*fingere*), meaning "to form."

It was Freud who first said that the finding of every object is actually a refinding of it.[9] Object relations theorists interpret this idea to mean that all adult loves and all adult hates are tinged with memories of earlier loves and hates. In fact, a large part of all experience is considered to be a melange of imitations or reactions to what went before. One way in which psychoanalysis increases a person's sense of meaning in life is by making her or him more aware of how the past is being repeated in the present. Therapy results in an increased breadth of response to what went before. The past is never really surmounted; instead, it is lived out in other ways. Thus psychoanalysis, like Goddess religion, participates in the myth of the eternal return through its ritual recall of history and by its stress on experiencing the deep past as alive in the seemingly flimsy present.

There are great differences between how the two philosophies approach the past. Analysis consists of formal, elaborate reflection on one person's personal past. In contrast, Goddess religion is a more diffuse effort to reanimate an earlier, pagan, collective connection to the natural world. Nevertheless, both philosophies look back in time for the purpose of healing the present. Neither has a strategy based on the promise of a utopian future in a "new world" imagined to be radically different.[10] There is no redemption expected to come in the form of a savior, or as a promised land, or from the benefits of scientific progress. For both thealogy and psychoanalysis, there is only the rather modest hope of improving life through reflection on the past. They have a common orientation toward making the world a better place—an orientation which differs significantly from most contemporary forward-looking approaches to human salvation.

Female Prehistory and the Deconstruction of the Phallus

Even more significant than their shared reverence for the deep past is the fact that both thealogy and object relations theory agree on what, or rather who, is the most important part of the past. Object relations theory departs from classical analytic theory by replacing Freud's keen interest in the father with an intense preoccupation with the mother. Like the Goddess movement in religion, object relations theory places a woman at the beginning of the universe and thus champions a shift from an interest in male symbols to a focus on female ones. Both ways of thinking pose a challenge to the importance of the father.

By stressing those ignored or suppressed portions of collective religious history which refer to female figures of power, thealogy chips away at the monolith constructed in patriarchal history. Even if particular facts or arguments about the history of Goddess worship are disputed, the work of writers such as

195

Merlin Stone, Marija Gimbutas, Savina Teubal, Charlene Spretnak, and others loosens the male monopoly on religious power.[11] To teach that Judaism and Christianity arose out of pagan cultural contexts which granted women a great deal of prominence, certainly in their mythologies and possibly in their hierarchies, is to teach that Judaism and Christianity had political motives for their early rejection and denigration of female imagery. This approach to religious history makes it possible for many people to see female imagery living on in dominant traditions. Women are there. Things female are there. But they have been inverted or cloaked in order to be appropriated by male phallic history and mythology.

According to hypotheses framed by researchers into Goddess religion, Yahweh grew to power as a jealous God whose followers smashed the icons of those who worshiped female divinities tied to nature. Gradually, holidays which were once understood as marking the seasonal cycles of "mother earth" became joined to accounts of male triumphs. The Exodus story obscured tales of the goddesses and their festivals of spring. The winter solstice became identified with a military victory instead of with the birth of the child of the Goddess. A harvest celebration thanking the mother deities for food became an occasion to read a male God's commandments.[12] As Christian symbolism became popular, Jesus replaced all the sons and lovers of the goddesses. He urged his followers to place more value on male words than on those "paps which gave thee suck."[13] In later centuries, a male clergy nearly succeeded in erasing the contribution of Christian women from recorded history.[14] Complete submission to male authority became the only appropriate role for women. All the deities that represented the great Goddess—the independent, often dangerous virgins and the lusty, powerful mothers—were reduced to one Virgin Mother, whose most celebrated utterance is "Let it be done to me according to thy Will."[15]

The Goddess movement proposes that sexual politics have formed the traditional religious myths of Western culture. Because Goddess sympathizers suspect that patriarchal symbols rest on a stratum that both suppresses and appropriates a female prehistory, they are led to question all the important rites and images of the dominant faiths. They wonder if the bar mitzvah might not be the glorified male counterpart of a ceremony marking the onset of menstruation.[16] They feel empathy and curiosity toward denigrated graven images such as the golden calf. They dare to ask just what was so awful about Jezebel, Vashti, and Lilith?[17] They look at the Father, Son, and Holy Ghost and see another trinity—Diana, Luna, and Hecate.

This awareness of a possible female background to the symbols and customs of male power creates psychological distance from those symbols and customs. By raising the suspicion that solid male institutions are not all they have seemed or, rather, are more than they have seemed, Goddess ideology loosens the grip of masculine symbols upon the contemporary imagination. Both the facts and the fantasies of the Goddess movement function to crack the edifice of patriarchy by encouraging the emergence of suppressed patterns of language, visions, dreams, and theories.

I find a similar subversion of male discourse and symbols in the work of certain female theorists of psychoanalysis. Melanie Klein writes that the male fear of castration is actually derived from earlier anxiety about the disappearance of the mother's breast. Klein thinks that each infant sees the breast as a part of his or her own body—a part that sometimes vanishes to cause great discomfort. The male child transfers this early experience

197

of bodily loss to his feelings about another physical protrusion, his penis.[18] Similarly, Klein believes that when penis-envy occurs in women, it leads back to a desire to possess the mother's breast. Thus, for her, the power behind the symbol of the penis in adulthood is explained by the earlier importance of the breast.[19]

More recently, Luce Irigaray presents another theory to account for the intense male fear of castration.[20] She suggests that the idea that a part of the body might be lost forever has its origin in the severing of the umbilical cord. Since a connection to the mother is lost when the umbilicus is snipped off, the cutting of the cord at the beginning of every life is traumatic. This event might well underlie all fears about the loss of pieces of the body. Irigaray's theory implies, I think, that for men, the penis may be the only way back to mother once the umbilical cord has been cut. While women have the option of closely identifying with their mothers, men's only hope of return lies in the penis. Since patriarchal culture restricts the ways in which men may be like their mothers, the penis becomes overvalued as the sole masculine tie to femininity.

The work of Melanie Klein and Luce Irigaray deconstructs the penis—that primary symbol of male domination. Their theories arouse the suspicion that the fabled organ might derive its power by evoking a connection to mother. Is phallic bravado a cover-up for the fact that castration has already occurred? Does it disguise the fact that the path to the mother— via the umbilicus and the breast—has already been cut off? The male compulsion to praise the penis is everywhere in men's writing. It appears in trashy novels such as those of Mickey Spillane, in better novels such as those of Norman Mailer, and in great theoretical works such as those of Sigmund Freud and Jacques Lacan. Could this unflagging interest have its root in the deep male desire to reconnect with the mother—a desire which expresses itself in a glorification of the only organ which can lead back to her?

By pointing to a female background behind the prominent male icons of both religion and psychology, the Goddess movement and object relations theory work to displace the father from his domination of the symbolic order. Both bodies of theory express and accelerate the slow erosion of male authoritarianism in Western culture.

A Shared Vision of the Human Being in Community

Another similarity between Goddess religion and object relations theory is that both stress the dependence of human beings on their communities. Unlike much patriarchal philosophy, which emphasizes individualism and self-determination, Goddess religion and object relations theory teaches that people are created in large part by their relationships.

For object relations analysts, the focus on human life in community derives from the significance which the theory places on infancy and early childhood. Babies or young children simply cannot exist without the constant care and supervision of at least one adult, who is usually a woman. A baby is thus never a solitary being. D. W. Winnicott calls attention to the mother-infant pair by insisting that "there is no such thing as a baby."[21] Margaret Mahler takes the fusion of mother and child to absurdity by referring to a child's mother as a personified environment. "The environment . . . extremely overanxious, consulted one doctor after another," Mahler writes.[22]

These two famous quotations dramatize one of the central tenets of object relations theory—namely, that the life experience of human beings is determined in large part by other human beings. Although this interdependence is most apparent in early life, the theory maintains that it is also true of adulthood. Joan Riviere describes our mutual construction of one another in adult life in this way:

> We tend to think of any one individual in isolation; it is a convenient fiction. We may isolate him physically, as in the analytic room; in two minutes we find that he has brought his world in with him, and that even before he set eyes on the analyst, he had developed inside himself an elaborate relation with him. There is no such thing as a single human being, pure and simple, unmixed with other human beings. Each personality is a world in himself, a company of many. That self, that life of one's own, which is in fact so precious though so casually taken for granted, is a composite structure which has been and is being formed and built up since the day of our birth out of countless never-ending influences and exchanges between ourselves and others. . . . These other persons are in fact therefore parts of ourselves. And we ourselves similarly have and have had effects and influence, intended or not, on all others who have an emotional relation to us, have loved or hated us. We are members one of another.[23]

To Riviere, being human means existing *in situ,* that is, in a nexus of relations with people past and present. She suggests that a truly autonomous person can exist only in theory—in an imagined parenthesis which excludes the animating context of history and emotions. Her words are an eloquent description of an object relations view of human nature: "We are members one of another."

There are several feminist theorists who are saying much the same thing as the object relations analysts. Human beings, say these theorists, are constructed in large part by their social, political, economic, and linguistic circumstances.[24] Thus, as Naomi Schemen phrases it, "questions of meaning and interpretation [in psychology and philosophy] cannot be answered in abstraction from a social setting."[25] This stress on the social context of experience actually extends the perspective of object relations theory which sometimes concentrates too narrowly on the social world as seen from a baby's perspective. To psychoanalysts, mother is the social context of baby, while to feminist theorists, mother and baby are both embedded in a bigger world. Object relations emphasizes the infant's immediate human environment, while feminist theory tries to understand the larger social conditions which make each particular human environment what it is. This exploration of the social world which constructs mothering is motivated by the feminist project of understanding women's experience in order to both learn from that experience and affect it for the better. From its early beginnings, feminist theory has been concerned with articulating the ways in which human lives, particularly women's lives, have been structured by the external world. "The personal is political" was an early slogan that has held true for the past two decades of feminist thought. The "personal," say feminists, is an artificial construct which should never be thought of as radically separate from public life. All spheres of human activity are related.

The Goddess movement, like object relations theory in particular and feminist theory in general, is concerned with expanding awareness of the conditions which make lives what they are. Thealogy, however, focuses on some other, nonhuman aspects of the context of life. The Goddess movement takes seriously the ancient pagan perception that human life is part of a larger web of life which includes all of nature. Like the ecology movement, thealogy sees human life in a dynamic planetary context which is determined by the state of the water, the soil, and the air. The entire earth is conceptualized as the body of the Goddess and thus is sacred. No part of the

201

ecosystem is separate from her, and thus no part of the material world is considered secular or profane. Starhawk, an eminent thealogian, describes the Goddess as existing in the complex connections of the entire universe. "Each individual self," she writes, "is linked by ties of blood and affection to the coven, which in turn is a part of the larger human community, the culture and society in which it is found, and that culture is part of the biological/geological community of Planet Earth and the cosmos beyond, the dance of being which we call Goddess."[26]

I suggest that the mutual concern of psychoanalysis and thealogy with articulating the context of human life arises because both philosophies center around the image of a powerful woman in the past. Since every human life begins in the body of a woman, the image of a woman, whether thought of as mother or as Goddess always points to an early history of connectedness: Mother-*mater*-matter-matrix. "Woman" is the stuff out of which all people are made. In the beginning was her flesh, and, after the beginning, she continues to suggest human historicity, to suggest human connection to and dependence upon the outside world. It is this deep memory of birth union, I think, which turns any serious reflection on women into a reflection on the interconnection of human beings with each other and with all the things which make up the body of the world. It is pre-birth experience and post-birth mothering which destine feminist theory to expand awareness of the context which supports everything human.

At a basic level, the image of woman is the image of human context—the image of human connection to the world. Object relations theory limits the image to mother and thus theorizes context somewhat narrowly as the mother-infant relationship. Thealogy extends the image to deity and thus envisions context more grandly as the planet as a whole. Both derive their insights into the matrices that support human life from an image of a woman-in-the-past. Classical Freudian psychoanalysis with its focus on an often absent *paterfamilias* and traditional religion with its focus on a father in heaven could never inspire similar reflection about the complex contingency of human existence.

Agreement that the Basis of Thought Lies in Fantasy

One aspect of the human context upon which both thealogians and analysts agree is fantasy. Both groups understand fantasy, or wish, as constituting the primary matrix for all mental processes.

In witchcraft, the cultivation of wishing pervades almost every practice. Goddess religion can often appear as "wishcraft" because it teaches women to use spells and rituals to express their hopes, ambitions, and desires. Much of the effectiveness of these "magical" practices can be explained by their ability to focus the mind and to mobilize willpower. Witches feel that a goal which can be visualized in detail is more likely to be a goal which can be reached. Thus they concentrate on representing wishes symbolically either in the form of physical objects such as amulets and talismans or in the choreography and incantations of ceremonies and rituals.

In addition to employing fantasy in religious practice, thealogians also use it to "do thealogy," that is, to theorize about the Goddess. Sometimes the idea of a matriarchy in the past is put forward as a wish about history—a desire to be realized in the present and future. Thealogians are fond of quoting

203

these lines of Monique Wittig from *Les Guérillères:* "There was a time when you were not a slave, remember. Try hard to remember. Or, failing that, invent." The wisdom of the words lies in the recognition that belief in a state of beneficence that existed in the past is an idea which empowers in the present. Wittig recommends that an invented past can be substituted for a remembered one. After all, she implies, faith is simply a very strong wish.

Some thealogians realize that their research into the past is motivated by their desire to improve women's lot in the present. "Most writers on contemporary Goddess religion, womanspirit or Witchcraft cite the past to offer a historical basis for the present traditions," Starhawk writes. But then she adds:

> I am not going to do that here. Historical points are always arguable, and while the past may serve us with models and myths, we need not look to it to justify the reemergence of the feminine principle. Whether or not women ever ruled in matriarchies, women are taking power today. Whether or not contemporary Witchcraft has its roots in the Stone Age, its branches reach into the future.[27]

Starhawk, like some others, understands that for any living religion, the importance of the past lies in how it is used in the present. She knows that her religion, just as all others, is based around wishes and hopes for power, comfort, influence, and justice.

Object relations theorists share the conviction that wish and fantasy are central to human enterprise.[28] Instead of separating "reality thinking" from "fantasy thinking," as did Freud and many of his followers, object relations analysts conceive of fantasy as the basis or context of all thinking.[29] What is felt to

204

be real in the inner, psychic world, they say, tends to be what is created in the external world. Fantasy is seen as creating the blueprint of a life.

Much to their credit, object relations theorists do not often take this idea to ridiculous lengths such as blaming the victim of a crime for wishing its occurrence. They do, however, use the idea of unconscious fantasy to explore character structure, ambition, and creativity. According to object relations theorists, people build their "real" worlds of work, friends, and family to correspond to their deepest inner expectations. These analysts therefore, like many witches, see the entire external, human world as something constructed upon a stratum of internal fantasy.

Unlike the witches, object relations analysts do not believe that willpower can control fantasy.[30] To the object relations analyst, the structure of a person's fantasy life is laid down in infancy and early childhood. Paula Heimann states the general position succinctly: "The earliest experiences lay the foundations for the type of response to people and events; those who have learned in infancy that frustration and anxiety can be quickly removed approach life with an optimistic attitude, and are capable of recovering from disappointments."[31] In object relations theory, a person's general attitude expresses the parameters of fantasies which have been sketched from the time of earliest infancy—a time when satisfaction depended on forces entirely outside each baby's control. Thus, to psychoanalysts, a person's attitude, inner world, and fantasy life are greatly influenced by her or his early environment and by the caregivers who shaped that environment. Analysts believe that a basic change in fantasy expression occurs only if something, such as analysis, effects a change in psychic dynamics. To them, fantasy is too much a product of personal history to be

205

seriously influenced by the rituals and spells employed by the Goddess worshipers.

Even though the analysts and the witches disagree about the malleability of fantasy, attitude, and expectation, they both maintain that the inner world of anticipation and wish is the basis of all human thought and action. Consciousness and directed rational thought are considered to be relatively superficial phenomena which derive from older, more encompassing unconscious structures.

I think these four parallels between Goddess religion and object relations theory have a significance beyond the particular disciplines which have so far addressed them. If the ways of thinking discussed here become more typical, not only of psychological and theological discourse, but also of other branches of study, then Western thought in general will become more embodied and more contextualized. The serious inclusion of women in any system of thought fosters reflection that is grounded in both the physical body and in the body politic. This focus on human contingency and historicity is in direct contrast to the way the Platonic theory of forms has structured most Western theology and philosophy.

The idea that the best things about the world are somehow not a part of the world extends far beyond Plato.[32] It exists in the work of philosophers like Hegel, who attributes influence to entities such as the Spirit and the Absolute. It exists in the work of analytic psychologists like Jung, who derives the motives of human behavior from immaterial essences called archetypes. And it exists in religions like Christianity, which places responsibility for the existence of the world in the hands of a God who exists apart from the world. Such philosophies, such psychologies, such religions will undergo radical change if they are pressured to discard the belief that the world is constructed by disembodied abstractions.

As women become more and more central to all branches of Western thought, the belief in transcendent entities will become less and less tenable. This is true, I suggest, because the transcendent, the immaterial, and the metaphysical is actually the embodied, the physical, and the female. It is the exclusion of things female from philosophy, psychology, and theology which has allowed these disciplines to construct notions of an abstract presence which creates the world and then controls it. To include women means to recognize the physical contingency of all thought and all creation.

Ancient mythology illustrates the fact that the world does indeed begin with a woman and that it is the memory of her which inspires later creative thought. Consider the *Enuma Elish,* the ancient Babylonian epic of creation. In the poem, the hero Marduk kills the monster Tiamat and forms the world from her body. The heavens, the stars, the seas, the rivers, and the land all begin as parts of her. A woman's body is the body of the world. Creative action in the world is depicted in the poem as aggressive use of a mother's body. Mother and world are presented as identical.[33]

The object relations work of Klein and Winnicott agrees with the cosmology of the *Enuma Elish*. Klein believes that infants experience their first acts of exploring the world as aggression against their mothers.[34] In contrast to Klein, Winnicott places much less stress on aggression as an early motive force. He thinks that babies become more involved with the world in direct proportion to the degree that they extend the sense of being with the mother to the greater environment. Winnicott considers the first objects (such as blankets and teddy bears) which stand for mother as "transitional" objects.

These objects, like mother, are felt to be both part of the child and part of the external world. In his view, culture, art, and religion are elaborations of transitional objects—constructions arising from the early sense of being able to use the world in the way that mother was used.[35]

Thus, in object relations theory as well as in some of the earliest Western mythology, human experience of the world as well as all reflection on it is understood as based on the early tie to a woman. The Platonic search for the immaterial, original world of disembodied forms is an inversion of the real quest in which all humans have been involved since babyhood—that of extending their physical, psychological, animal presence into the material world. The quest is motivated more by a desire to reexperience and elaborate a union with matter, with mother, than it is to escape the embrace of the physical world. Plato has it backwards; the search for the wholly transcendent is, historically and psychologically, the search for the remembered state of union with the wholly immanent.

In Greek mythology, the image which tells the truth (psychologically and historically) about the human drives to explore the world and to create culture is that of the Muses, the nine daughters of Olympian Zeus and the Titaness Mnemosyne, Memory. The Muses are said to inspire mortals with their voices. They sing to those they love and bestow talents which make these humans happy, wise, and respected.

Surely the image of the Muses is derived from infancy and early childhood. This is the time when the sound of a woman's voice means nearly everything to nearly everyone. It signals the arrival of food, of warmth, of comfort, and of entertainment. She is heard before she is seen and that sound, because it is linked with the anticipation of good things to come, sparks the infant imagination. A woman's voice focused the

208

attention of most babies in ancient Greece just as it focuses the attention of most babies in the contemporary world. No wonder that the Muses, the primary image of inspiration in Western thought, always work their magic through female voices.[36]

Object relations theory and ancient mythology both insist on the connection between the memory of the ties to a woman's body and the human desires to explore, to theorize, and to conceptualize the world. The Platonic tradition denies this connection by denigrating what is merely physical, by claiming that all knowledge is motivated by bodiless forms. The centuries-old tendency to exclude women from arenas of learning called "higher" is probably a social dramatization of this denial. Women and matter have been repressed in our intellectual traditions when, in truth, they are at the origins of all reflection.

That which has been repressed is now returning. The contemporary focus on women in all areas of creative thought—in all domains of the Muses—means that the sources of thought itself will become clearer. This is the real significance of the return of the Goddess. When theology becomes thealogy, the metaphysical comes home to the physical.

Conclusion

I have always been fascinated by the statues that Michelangelo sculpted toward the end of his life. They are human figures which are still embedded in the rough stone, continuous with their backgrounds, in the material from which they were created. Each formed figured thus illuminates the substance that forms it. I think theory should be like this—theory should illuminate more and more of the body, more and more of the context in which we theorize. The goal I have imagined for myself in this work is that of grasping the body in theory with theory.

By body, I do not mean the body as exaggeratedly praised by many back-to-nature movements. I distrust natural food, fiber, and medicine fanatics almost as much as I do born-again religious zealots. The smiles of both sorts of devotees hide anger, I think. I suspect that many back-to-nature movements scapegoat technology by making it represent all the impurities of self and world they find so confusing. The answers of some back-to-nature movements disguise too many problems. We need to learn to see more complexity in our environment, and not to energetically reject large portions of our world. I see body as including nature as part of itself. I do not want to think of body as an isolated "pure nature" which is separated from a total environmental context.

What I am calling body stands in contrast to the notion of transcendence in traditional theology. Transcendence is a wish for something beyond body, beyond time, and beyond specific relationships to life. Such a notion of perfect safety involves negation of this world and is probably motivated by a characteristically (but not exclusively) male fear of being merged with matter. Theologians envision salvation as up, out, and beyond, and call this hoped-for state of dissociation the ultimate reality. In fact, it is no reality at all but rather a death-wish, which Christianity aptly symbolizes by a male dying on a cross. In the course of Christian history, men have much preferred to promote this image of suffering and agony instead of any image of love and playfulness such as that of Mary with her baby. The crucifixion is therefore now the central image of modern Christianity. And the medium is the message.

The particularly male obsession with a dying man dominates and limits the work of most male theologians. When they look at this world, these men tend to find it insufficient, disappointing, and even threatening. It is the cross to which they are nailed. Because daily life is so unsatisfying, another world is required—the transcendent world of God. Often, many male theologians focus on life after death. Note how such issues do not fascinate feminist theologians who are more concerned with hopes for life before death. Life after death is an issue that is symptomatic of structures of thought which reject the richness and depth of the physical, social universe in which we live.

It might be possible to have a concept of transcendence which is not deathlike. A transcendence with body, a transcendence that is life-oriented, would involve feelings of con-

211

nection instead of separation. It might be possible for transcendence to refer to a state of knowing oneself to be part of other human lives—to knowing that one's life is linked with other lives. Feeling part of an enormous effort at social reform such as the women's movement has been an experience of transcendence for many of us. The feeling of participation in the body politic not only provides a tie to a present collective community, but also links our lives to the lives of those who lived before us and those who will live after us. Such transcendence is a quality of the here and now—a feeling that is part of the present moment and that provides a significant tie to human history and society. It fosters feelings of being alive. It is far-removed from the deathlike hope for a static detachment which patriarchal theology presents as paradise. One of the tasks of feminist thealogy is to name the out-of-body fantasies of traditional theology as the death-wishes they are. Our visions of happiness, of peace, of contentment must be as embodied as life itself. To extol salvation as something other than a human condition is to envy the dead, unfeeling presence of machines. The only transcendence worth working for is one based on an awareness of our own contingency.

I want to emphasize that body is much more than dumb flesh. Bodily experience has a complexity that is often denied. Human bodies experience everything—even the most specific sensation—in a complex context of memory and wish. If our theories and social practices are to foster an awareness of body, they must show reverence for those parts of physicality which we usually call emotions. Much of modern culture treats our emotions as if they were separable from our physical selves. Hospitals, for example, are notorious for treating bodies like machines with defects to be fixed as if they were broken parts on an assembly line. The same is true of many modern sports in which athletes train to turn their bodies into mechanisms to perform tasks with absolute perfection. Medicine and sports are examples of practices that often disembody the body and turn it into a thing or an instrument. The awareness of body that I want to see would entail sensitivity to feelings, to histories, and to the physical presence of friends and families. Our bodies should be understood as the sum of all our particular situations as created by a complex web of physical, social, emotional, and historical contingencies.

I want a feminist notion of body to expand our sense of the body politic. Survival probably depends on fostering empathy among races and cultures. Feminism has a part to play here by exposing the objectification of all groups which are treated as "others." In order to tolerate a more realistic relationship with more and more people, we must learn to stop idealizing and vilifying each other. We have to become much more sophisticated in our understanding of the human dynamics of envy and hatred.

This brings me to the last factor I want to see included in theories based in the body. I want to see body include what psychoanalysts have called the unconscious. Theories with body should be theories which take account of rage and desire—they should be theories which put our conscious awareness in the context of our unconscious wishes and fears. They should be theories which foster awareness of the so-called baser drives of all human beings.

Religion has not been very good at taking account of human emotions. Bodily loves and hates either have been projected onto other groups considered ungodly or have been repressed in the name of goodness, godliness, and spirituality. The result is that religion has functioned to cut us off from essential parts of ourselves.

The very words that we use to describe religious feelings portray those feelings as disembodied. For example, a typical definition of "spiritual" reads as follows:

1. of the spirit or the soul, often in a religious or moral aspect, as distinguished from the body.
2. of, from, or concerned with the intellect, or what is often thought of as the better or higher part of the mind.
3. of, or consisting of spirit; not corporeal.
4. characterized by the ascendancy of the spirit; showing much refinement of thought and feeling.[1]

In accordance with these definitions, "spirituality" is defined as "spiritual character, quality, or nature: opposed to sensuality, worldliness" and "the fact or state of being incorporeal."[2]

The "women's spirituality movement" is a phrase often applied to contemporary feminist religious thought. But is spirituality an appropriate word for this type of thinking? Or is it a limiting word—a word which implies that some parts of life are elevated and some are not? Doesn't spirituality imply that some things are sacred and some profane? Doesn't spirituality give us a judgmental hierarchical notion of which experiences are worth having?

Much feminist thought about religion goes deeper than the concept of spirituality. It expands our sensibility and awareness of life without idealizing incorporeality or praising states of being that are radically set apart from typical experience. It is thus better characterized as being about body than being about spirit. Perhaps our theories are developing faster than some of the language we use to describe them. Perhaps our words have not yet caught up with us. Spirituality might be one word which now limits us in our conceptions of what we are doing by mystifying the direction of our theories.

However, I am also afraid that the word "body" is already on the way to becoming a mystified abstraction in the jargon of postmodern discourse. Perhaps emphasizing the *body* obscures the fact that our sense of physicality is in large part determined by our day-to-day relationships with one another. For this reason, I probably will not stress the term again in future work. Words, I think, should be discarded as soon as they begin to conceal what they ought to illuminate. Our terminology should be flexible in order to bring more and more of human experience and possibility into the range of our theory.

Notes

Introduction

1. See, for example, Russell Jacoby, *The Last Intellectuals: American Culture in the Age of Academe* (New York: Basic Books, 1987); Brian Fawcett, *Cambodia: A Book for People Who Find Television Too Slow* (Vancouver: Talonbooks, 1986); and also Janice Newson and Howard Buchbinder, *The University Means Business* (Toronto: Garamond Press, 1988).

2. See Ella Freeman Sharpe, "Psycho-Physical Problems Revealed in Language: An Examination of Metaphor," in *Collected Papers on Psycho-Analysis* (New York: Brunner/Mazel, 1978).

3. Christiane Rochefort, "Are Women Writers Still Monsters?" in *New French Feminisms: An Anthology,* ed. Elaine Marks and Isabelle de Courtivron (New York: Schocken Books, 1981), p. 183.

4. John 1:14, *The Holy Bible,* King James Version.

Chapter 1

1. See Susan Sontag's essay "The Imagination of Disaster," in *Against Interpretation* (New York: Dell Publishing Co., 1961), for the classic analysis of apocalypse in science fiction movies.

2. Susan Sontag, *On Photography* (New York: Farrar, Straus and Giroux, 1978).

3. Hélène Cixous, "The Laugh of the Medusa," trans. Keith Cohen and Paula Cohen, in *New French Feminisms,* ed. Elaine Marks and Isabelle de Courtivron (New York: Schocken Books, 1981), p. 263.

4. Sherry Turkle, *The Second Self: Computers and the Human Spirit* (New York: Simon and Schuster, 1984), p. 6.

5. Ibid., p. 322.

6. Ibid., p. 20.

7. Matter comes from the Latin root *mater,* meaning mother. As will become clear throughout this book, I find this derivation important. Transcendence in Western thought is, in some sense, always transcendence from women.

8. Adrian Stokes, *Reflections on the Nude* (London: Tavistock Publications, 1967), p. 49. Many of the writings of Annie Dillard show how involvement with the natural world can lead us to such sanity. See, for example, *Pilgrim at Tinker Creek* (New York: Harper and Row, Perennial Library, 1985 [1974]).

9. Stokes, *Reflections on the Nude,* p. 7.

10. Ibid., p. 11.

11. Ibid., p. 36.

12. Ibid., p. 33.

13. Tom Robbins, *Still Life with Woodpecker* (New York: Bantam Books, 1980), p. 271.

14. For a good discussion of why a "self" can never be wholly autonomous, see Catherine Keller, *From a Broken Web: Separation, Sexism, and the Self* (Boston: Beacon Press, 1986).

15. See Bob Schacochis, "In Deepest Gringolandia—Mexico: The Third World as Tourist Theme Park," *Harper's* 279, no. 1670 (July 1989); pp. 42–50, for a less optimistic view of Western interest in the Third World.

16. Todd Gitlin, "Postmodernism Defined, At Last!" *Utne Reader,* July/August 1989, pp. 52–61.

Chapter 2

1. Norman O. Brown, *Life against Death: The Psychoanalytical Meaning of History* (New York: Random House, 1959), p. 158. For another feminist approach to Brown's work, see Nancy Chodorow, *Feminism and Psychoanalytic Theory* (New Haven: Yale University Press, 1989).

2. Susan Sontag, *Against Interpretation* (New York: Dell Publishing Co., 1961), pp. 258–59.

3. Brown, *Life against Death,* p. 313.

4. Ibid., p. 144.

5. Ibid.

6. Ibid., p. 316.

7. Ibid., p. 173.

8. It is amusing to note that in the 1959 edition of *Life against Death,* the word "shit" is never printed. Words such as "feces" and "excrement" are used instead. In the one instance when the word is necessary in the text (on

page 189), it is discreetly hyphenated like this: "sh—". Printing, it seems, has enjoyed a lessening of repression since the publication of *Life against Death*.

9. Ruskin, *Unto This Last,* in *Works* 17:85, as cited in Brown, *Life against Death*, p. 253; see also Herman E. Daly and John B. Cobb, Jr., *For the Common Good: Redirecting the Economy toward Community, the Environment, and a Sustainable Future* (Boston: Beacon Press, 1989).

10. Brown, *Life against Death*, p. 236.

11. See, for example, Evelyn Fox Keller, *Reflections on Gender and Science* (New Haven: Yale University Press, 1985), and *A Feeling for the Organism: The Life and Work of Barbara McClintock* (New York: Freeman, 1983). The work of Geraldine Finn has been a major influence on my own thinking about science and technology. See her "Women and the Ideology of Science," *Our Generation* 15, no. 1.

12. Brown, *Life against Death,* p. 232.

13. Ibid., p. 295.

14. Ibid., pp. 291–92.

15. Ernest Becker, *The Denial of Death* (New York: Free Press, Macmillan Publishing Co., 1973), p. 261.

16. Dorothy Dinnerstein, *The Mermaid and the Minotaur: Sexual Arrangements and Human Malaise* (New York: Harper and Row, 1976), p. 184.

17. Becker, *The Denial of Death*, p. 285.

18. Ibid., p. 276.

19. Ibid., p. 233.

20. Ibid., p. 311.

21. Ibid., p. 34.

22. Norman O. Brown, *Love's Body* (New York: Random House, 1966), p. vi.

23. James Joyce, *Finnegans Wake* (New York: Viking Press, 1966), p. 497, as cited in Norman O. Brown, *Closing Time* (New York: Random House, 1973), p. 109.

24. Brown, *Love's Body*, p. 259.

25. Joan Riviere, "The Unconscious Phantasy of an Inner World," 358–59, as cited in Brown, *Love's Body*, p. 147. For more on our construction of each other's lives, see "The Return of the Goddess," chapter 12 of this volume.

26. Brown, *Love's Body*, p. 227.

27. Ibid., p. 249.

28. Ibid.

29. Ibid., p. 260.

30. Ibid.

31. Ibid., p. 183. Brown quotes Blake (*Marriage of Heaven and Hell*) and Danielou (*Origen*) in this passage.

32. Hélène Cixous and Catherine Clément, *The Newly Born Woman*, trans. Betsy Wing (Minneapolis: University of Minnesota Press, 1986).

33. Julia Kristeva, "Stabat Mater," in *The Kristeva Reader*, trans. Leon S. Roudiez, ed. Toril Moi (New York: Columbia University Press, 1986), pp. 161–85.

34. See, for example, Luce Irigaray, "The 'Mechanics' of Fluids," in *This Sex Which Is Not One*, trans. Catherine Porter (Ithaca: Cornell University Press, 1985), pp. 106–18.

Even Jane Gallop, who in many ways writes as the father's daughter, does not imitate the veiled detachment of the father she loves so well. She is intensely present in her books, confessional and flirtatious. She thus achieves an embodied, if narcissistic, prose. See Jane Gallop, *The Daughter's Seduction: Feminism and Psychoanalysis,* (Ithaca: Cornell University Press, 1982), and *Thinking Through the Body* (New York: Columbia University Press, 1988). In *Thinking Through the Body,* Gallop continues to write as a *femme fatale.* However, her focus on authors who depict the abuse and torture of children and adolescents reveals an interest in abused young bodies as well as seductive ones. Perhaps Gallop's exhibitionism might have its roots in experiences she has yet to reveal in her writing.

35. An excellent argument for the need of better contextualizing Western theology and philosophy can be found in Catherine Keller's *From a Broken Web: Separation, Sexism, and the Self* (Boston: Beacon Press, 1986.)

36. Nelle Morton, "Hearing to Speech," in *The Journey Is Home* (Boston: Beacon Press, 1985), pp. 202–9.

37. Elisabeth Schüssler-Fiorenza, *In Memory of Her: A Feminist Theological Reconstruction of Christian Origins* (New York: Crossroad, 1983).

38. See Carol P. Christ, *Diving Deep and Surfacing: Women Writers on Spiritual Quest,* 2d ed. (Boston: Beacon Press, 1986), and *Laughter of Aphrodite: Reflections on a Journey to the Goddess* (New York: Harper and Row, 1987); Christine Downing, *The Goddess: Mythological Representations of the Feminine* (New York: Crossroad, 1984); Starhawk, *The Spiral Dance: A Rebirth of the Ancient Religion of the Great Goddess* (San Francisco: Harper and Row, 1979), and *Dreaming the Dark: Magic, Sex, and Politics* (Boston: Beacon Press, 1982). For a fine recent collection of writings on the women's spirituality movement, see Judith Plaskow and Carol Christ, eds., *Weaving the Visions: New Patterns in Feminist Spirituality* (New York: Harper and Row, 1989).

Chapter 3

1. For some other psychoanalytic reflections on football, see Childe Herald's essay, "Freud and Football," in *Reader in Comparative Religion: An Anthropological Approach,* 2d ed., ed. William A. Lessa and Evon Z. Vogt (New York: Harper and Row, 1965), pp. 250–52.

2. Sigmund Freud, *The Standard Edition of the Complete Psychological Works of Sigmund Freud,* ed. James Strachey, 24 vols. (London: Hogarth Press, 1953–74), 23: 190n. 1.

3. Melanie Klein, "Early Analysis," in *Love, Guilt, and Reparation and Other Works, 1921–1945* (New York: Delacorte Press, 1975), p. 86.

4. Tom Robbins, *Still Life with Woodpecker* (New York: Bantam Books, 1980), p. 136.

5. Ibid., p. 141.

6. Luce Irigaray, *This Sex Which Is Not One,* trans. Catherine Porter (Ithaca: Cornell University Press, 1985).

Chapter 4

1. Luce Irigaray, *This Sex Which Is Not One,* trans. Catherine Porter (New York: Cornell University Press, 1985); and Mary O'Brien, *The Politics of Reproduction* (London: Routledge and Kegan Paul, 1981).

2. For a challenge to "goyim-bashing," see Nan Fink, *Tikkun: A Bi-Monthly Jewish Critique of Politics, Culture, and Society* 4, no. 2 (March/April 1989): 7.

3. I am referring to W. Gunther Plaut's editorial which appeared in the *Globe and Mail* (Toronto) on January 3, 1984.

4. Luce Irigaray's work is often cited to support the idea that women's desires are essentially plural.

5. Audre Lorde, *Sister/Outsider* (Trumansburg, N.Y.: Crossing Press, 1984), p. 123.

6. Not every feminist would agree with me about a global mission for the women's movement. Some women have set their sights on other goals. For example, Susan Weidman Schneider, the author of *Jewish and Female* (New York: Simon and Schuster, 1984), argues that Jews should embrace feminism in order to make Jewish men and Jewish women more appealing to one another. If more Jews were more flexible about sex roles, she says, then fewer Jews would be tempted to find relief from Jewish gender stereotypes by marrying outside the community. In a statement made at Ottawa's Jewish Community Centre in January 1985, Weidman Schneider said that al-

though she finds nothing wrong with the goyim, it is a fact that "we all feel more comfortable with people like ourselves." In no way does Weidman Schneider urge feminism to extend this sense of community to include people "unlike ourselves." She thus envisages what I consider a wrong-headed goal for Jewish feminism, that is, the maintenance of a strong tribal identity.

7. Margaret Atwood, *You Are Happy* (Toronto: Oxford University Press, 1974), p. 39.

Chapter 5

1. See my articles "A Feminist Critique of Jung," *Signs* 2, no. 2 (Winter 1976): 443–49; "Feminism and Jungian Theory," *Anima* 3, no. 2 (Spring 1977): 14–17; *Changing of the Gods: Feminism and the End of Traditional Religions* (Boston: Beacon Press, 1979), pp. 54–64. An earlier essay on the evolution of the concept of archetype in Jungian theory is "Archetypal Theory after Jung," in *Spring 1975* (Zürich: Spring Publications, 1975), pp. 199–220.

2. Plato, *Apology,* trans. Hugh Tredennick, *Dialogues of Plato,* 30a–b, p. 16, as cited by Elizabeth V. Spelman, "Woman as Body: Ancient and Contemporary Views," *Feminist Studies* 8, no. 1 (Spring 1982): 111.

3. C. G. Jung, *The Collected Works of C. G. Jung,* ed. William G. McGuire et al., trans. R. F. C. Hull, Bollingen Series 20, 20 vols. (Princeton: Princeton University Press, 1954–79), 9 (1): 78–79.

4. Ibid., 8: 215.

5. Ibid., pp. 213, 215.

6. Ibid., p. 216.

7. Ibid., pp. 214, 216.

8. Ibid., 9 (1): 44.

9. Ibid., p. 79.

10. Sigmund Freud, *The Standard Edition of the Complete Psychological Works of Sigmund Freud,* ed. James Strachey, 24 vols. (London: Hogarth Press, 1953–74), 14: 60–62.

11. Norman O. Brown, *Life against Death: The Psychoanalytical Meaning of History* (New York: Random House, 1959), p. xi.

12. Ibid., p. 281.

13. Ibid., p. 284.

14. See also "Reviewing a Mentor: The Concept of Body in the Work of Norman O. Brown," chapter 2 in this volume.

15. See, for example, Lynne White, "The Religious Roots of Our Ecological Crisis," *Science* 155 (1967): 1203–1207. Also Elizabeth Dodson Gray, *Why the Green Nigger?* (Wellesley: Roundtable Press, 1979).

16. See, for example, Elizabeth V. Spelman, "Woman as Body: Ancient and Contemporary Views," *Feminist Studies* 8, no. 1 (Spring 1982): 109–31.

17. See Susan Griffin, *Women and Nature* (New York: Harper and Row, 1978).

18. Simone de Beauvoir, *The Second Sex,* trans. and ed. H. M. Parshley (New York: Alfred A. Knopf, 1952), p. 239.

19. Ibid., p. 685.

20. Spelman, "Woman as Body," p. 121.

21. Dorothy Dinnerstein, *The Mermaid and the Minotaur: Sexual Arrangements and Human Malaise* (New York: Harper and Row, 1976), p. 162.

22. Ibid., p. 162.

23. Ibid., p. 130.

24. Ibid., p. 218.

25. Nancy Chodorow, *The Reproduction of Mothering* (Berkeley: University of California Press, 1978).

26. Adrienne Rich, *Of Woman Born* (New York: Bantam Books, 1976), p. 21.

27. Ibid., p. 292.

28. Ibid., p. 290. For a recent effort in this direction, see Jane Gallop, *Thinking Through the Body* (New York: Columbia University Press, 1988).

29. Shulamith Firestone, *The Dialectic of Sex: The Case for Feminist Revolution* (New York: Bantam Books, 1971), p. 44. See also "'The Same Stuff': The Talking Cure of Feminism and Psychoanalysis," chapter 9 of this volume.

30. Freud, *Standard Edition,* 23: 300.

31. Ibid., p. 152.

32. Ibid., 20: 200.

33. Ibid., 22: 95.

34. Ibid., 14: 78.

35. Ibid., 22: 221.

36. Ibid., 14: 177.

37. James Hillman, *Revisioning Psychology* (New York: Harper and Row, 1975), p. 173. See also "Body and Psyche in the Work of James Hillman," chapter 7 in this volume.

38. D. W. Winnicott, "Mind and Its Relation to the Psyche-Soma," in *Through Paediatrics to Psycho-Analysis* (London: Hogarth Press and the Institute of Psycho-Analysis, 1978), p. 254.

39. Hillman, *Revisioning Psychology,* p. x.
40. Winnicott, "Mind and Its Relation to the Psyche-Soma," p. 243. For a discussion of intellectualization in Winnicott, see Jane Flax, *Thinking Fragments* (Berkeley: University of California Press, 1990), pp. 89–132.
41. C. G. Jung, *Memories, Dreams, Reflections* (New York: Random House, 1961), p. 18. See also "Looking at Jung Looking at Himself: A Psychoanalytic Rereading of *Memories, Dreams, Reflections,*" chapter 8 in this volume.
42. Spelman, "Woman as Body."
43. Melanie Klein, *The Psycho-Analysis of Children* (New York: Dell Publishing Co., 1975), p. 171. See also "Anger in the Body: The Impact of Idealization on Human Development and Religion," chapter 10 of this volume.
44. Adrienne Rich, from "Two Songs," as quoted in Spelman, "Woman as Body," p. 109.

Chapter 6

This essay was originally presented as a talk to the C. G. Jung Society of Montreal on March 13, 1987.

1. For a more detailed account of the development of archetypal theory, see my article, "Archetypal Theory after Jung," *Spring 1975* (Zürich: Spring Publications, 1975), pp. 199–220. On the theme of revising archetypal theory to better describe women's experience, see *Feminist Archetypal Theory: Interdisciplinary Revisions of Jungian Thought,* ed. Estella Lauter and Carol Schreier Rupprecht (Knoxville: University of Tennessee Press, 1985).

2. In her essay, "The Common Language of Women's Dreams: Colloquy of Mind and Body," in *Feminist Archetypal Theory,* pp. 187–219, Carol Schreier Rupprecht describes Jungian theory as unifying mind and body. I think Rupprecht places too much emphasis on some of Jung's scattered remarks about the unity of mind and body in order to portray his theories as liberating for women. Because Jungian theory does not lead to the analysis of the human circumstances that support the oppression of women, it cannot, I think, be revised to suit feminist goals.

3. See "Looking at Jung Looking at Himself: A Psychoanalytic Rereading of *Memories, Dreams, Reflections,*" chapter 8 in this volume.

4. C. G. Jung, *The Collected Works of C. G. Jung,* ed. William McGuire et al., trans. R. F. C. Hull, Bollingen Series 20, 20 vols. (Princeton: Princeton University Press, 1954–79), 10: 117–18.

5. Ibid., pp. 46–47. I have discussed other remarks Jung made about blacks and women in *Changing of the Gods: Feminism and the End of Tradi-*

224

tional Religions (Boston: Beacon Press, 1979), pp. 54–71, and in *Signs: Journal of Women in Culture and Society* 3, no. 3 (Spring 1978): 724–26.

6. See "On the Attack in the *Saturday Review of Literature*," in *C. G. Jung Speaking: Interviews and Encounters,* ed. William McGuire and R. F. C. Hull (Princeton: Princeton University Press, 1977), pp. 194–95.

7. Ibid., pp. 194–95.

8. Maya Deren, *Divine Horsemen: The Voodoo Gods of Haiti* (New York: Dell Publishing Co., 1970), p. 21.

9. Jung, *Collected Works,* 9 (1): 79.

10. Ibid.

11. Roland Barthes, *Mythologies,* trans. and ed. Annette Lavers (New York: Hill and Wang, 1972), p. 110, as cited by Julia Kristeva in *Desire in Language,* ed. Leon S. Roudiez (New York: Columbia University Press, 1980), p. 103.

Chapter 7

This essay was presented as a paper in 1983 at the meeting of the American Academy of Religion in Dallas, Texas. The session was titled "Directions from the Work of James Hillman."

1. Masud Khan, *Alienation in Perversion* (New York: International Universities Press, 1979), p. 226. In reviews of his work and in his obituaries, several writers have pointed out that Khan's later work became distorted and sprinkled with anti-Semitic ravings. Khan seems to have been prone to mental illness near the end of his life. See, for example, Janet Malcolm's review of Khan's last book, *The Long Wait and Other Psychoanalytic Narratives* in the *New York Times Book Review,* April 9, 1989, p. 25.

2. Khan, *Alienation in Perversion,* p. 226.

3. James Hillman, *Inter Views* (New York: Harper and Row, 1983), p. 155.

4. Ibid., p. 90.

5. Ibid., p. 144.

6. James Hillman, *Archetypal Psychology: A Brief Account* (Dallas: Spring Publications, 1983), p. 13.

7. Ibid., p. 3.

8. Hillman, *Inter Views,* p. 145.

9. See, for example, D. W. Winnicott, "Mind and Its Relations to the Psyche-Soma," in *Through Paediatrics to Psycho-Analysis* (London: Hogarth Press and the Institute of Psycho-Analysis, 1978), p. 244. See also "Arche-

typal Theory and the Separation of Mind and Body: Reason Enough to Turn to Freud?" chapter 5 in this volume.

10. D. W. Winnicott, *Playing and Reality* (New York: Penguin Books, 1971), p. 119.

11. James Hillman, "*Anima Mundi*: The Return of the Soul to the World," in *Spring 1982* (Dallas: Spring Publications), p. 89.

12. James Hillman, *Healing Fiction* (Tarrytown, N.Y.: Station Hill Press, 1983), p. 36.

13. Hillman, *Archetypal Psychology*, p. 17.

14. James Hillman, *Revisioning Psychology* (New York: Harper and Row, 1975), p. 173.

15. Hillman, *Archetypal Psychology*, p. 17.

16. Ibid., p. 36.

17. Tom Robbins, *Still Life with Woodpecker* (New York: Bantam Books, 1980), p. 156.

18. I note that in some of James Hillman's most recent works, the concept of psyche is not emphasized. In a wonderful lecture, "The Elephant in the Garden of Eden," sponsored by the C. G. Jung Society of Montreal on May 5, 1989, Hillman spoke more about "styles of imagining" than he did about psyche. A fine collection presenting the range of Hillman's thought is *A Blue Fire: Selected Writings by James Hillman*, edited by Thomas Moore (New York: Harper and Row, 1989).

Chapter 8

1. In his book, *Jung in Context: Modernity and the Making of a Psychology* (Chicago: University of Chicago Press, 1979), Peter Homans illuminates the evolution of Jung's thought by emphasizing the intellectual and religious milieux in which Jung lived and worked. Homans's work is valuable because it contextualizes Jung's thought, even though to my mind, he does not pay enough attention to Jung's early life.

2. Aniela Jaffé in C. G. Jung, *Memories, Dreams, Reflections*, ed. Aniela Jaffé, trans. Richard and Clara Winston, rev. ed. (New York: Vintage Books, 1963), p. vi. Subsequent references to *Memories* appear parenthetically in the text. All citations are from this edition of the work.

3. In his 1964 review of *Memories*, D. W. Winnicott writes that only the first three chapters of the autobiography are "the book." See *International Journal of Psycho-Analysis* 45 (1964): 450–55.

4. Winnicott thinks that keeping secrets remained important for Jung throughout much of his life (ibid., p. 452).

5. Winnicott remarks on how Jung's interpretation "lacks any attempt to relate this dream with four-year-old Jung's instinctual life." (ibid., p. 453).

6. Marie-Louise von Franz, *C. G. Jung: His Myth in Our Time,* trans. William H. Kennedy (Boston: Little Brown and Co., 1975), p. 15.

7. Ibid., p. 15.

8. Henri F. Ellenberger, *The Discovery of the Unconscious: The History and Evolution of Dynamic Psychiatry* (New York: Basic Books, 1970), p. 662.

9. Perhaps the "choking sensation" might also be traced to the sexual abuse to which he refers in a letter in Freud. See notes 15 and 18 below.

10. It is perhaps not going too far to interpret Jung's lifelong effort to establish a psychology which would replace religion as a further development of this early vision of successful competition with his father.

11. A possible relevant comment is Jung's remark that he avoided winning games in school. He felt more comfortable being in second place. Jung, *Memories, Dreams, Reflections,* p. 43.

12. C. G. Jung, *Answer to Job* in *The Collected Works of C. G. Jung,* ed. William McGuire et al., trans. R. F. C. Hull, Bollingen Series 20, 20 vols. (Princeton: Princeton University Press, 1954–79), 11: 366.

13. Ibid., p. 408.

14. Ibid., pp. 410–11. See also "Anger in the Body: The Impact of Idealization on Human Development and Religion," in chapter 10 in this volume.

15. These comments assume a deeper significance in the context of Jung's sexual abuse as a child, which I shall discuss shortly. See *The Freud/Jung Letters: The Correspondence between Sigmund Freud and Carl Jung,* ed. William McGuire, trans. Ralph Manheim and R. F. C. Hull, Bollingen Series 44 (Princeton: Princeton University Press, 1974), p. 95. His assault by a trusted adult might have reminded Jung of the dream imagery in which someone had "the impudence to exhibit a phallus so nakedly."

16. Ibid.

17. Demaris S. Wehr, *Jung and Feminism: Liberating Archetypes* (Boston: Beacon Press, 1987), p. 71.

18. I am grateful to Dr. Dean Eyre for calling my attention to the factors which indicate that Jung might have been sexually abused by his father. He referred me to S. Ferenczi's 1933 essay "Confusion of Tongues between Adults and the Child," in *Final Contributions to the Problems and Methods of*

Psycho-Analysis (New York: Brunner/Mazel, 1980), pp. 156–57. Ferenczi's discussion of the psychological confusion existing in families in which abuse occurs seems relevant to what Jung writes about his childhood.

19. Ellenberger, *The Discovery of the Unconscious,* p. 662.

20. See also Anthony Storr, *C. G. Jung* (New York: Viking Press, 1973), pp. 1–2. Storr accepts Jung's explanation of his difficulties with his father.

21. Masud Khan, *Alienation in Perversion* (New York: International Universities Press, 1979).

22. Laurens van der Post made this remark during his lecture at the Jung conference held at the University of Notre Dame in 1976.

23. John Freeman and C. G. Jung, "The 'Face to Face' Interview," in *C. G. Jung Speaking: Interviews and Encounters,* ed. William McGuire and R. F. C. Hull (Princeton: Princeton University Press, 1977), p. 426. See also Storr, *C. G. Jung,* p. 2.

24. Freeman and Jung, "The 'Face to Face' Interview," p. 427.

25. I also interpret the manikin Jung kept in a box in the attic as an example of a fantasy expressing a need for protection (see *Memories,* pp. 21–23).

26. Ellenberger, *The Discovery of the Unconscious,* p. 669.

27. Jung himself linked his ambivalent feelings toward Freud with the fact of his sexual abuse by a trusted older man. (See notes 15 and 18 above.) See also Vincent Brome's discussion of this in *Jung: Man and Myth* (New York: Atheneum, 1981), pp. 98–99; and Christine Downing, *Myths and Mysteries of Same-Sex Love* (New York: Continuum, 1989), pp. 92–104.

28. Aniela Jaffé mentioned this to me and the journalist Diana Lurie during an interview at Jaffé's home in Zürich in 1974.

29. C. G. Jung, "Marriage as a Psychological Relationship," in *Collected Works,* 17: 196.

30. Robert Smith, of the Department of Philosophy and Religion at Trenton State College, calls attention to this aspect of Jung's psychology in his unpublished paper "Deepseated Ambivalence toward the Feminine: Jung's Psychology as Maternally Oriented."

31. C. G. Jung, "Men, Women, and God," in *C. G. Jung Speaking,* p. 248.

32. Ellenberger, *The Discovery of the Unconscious,* p. 658.

33. According to Vincent Brome, Jung's cousin, Hélène Preiswerk, the medium who became the subject of Jung's doctoral dissertation, had a second personality named Ivènes, whose behavior was a marked contrast to what was usual for the young woman (Brome, *Jung,* pp. 67–68). Perhaps Jung's interest in Hélène had its precedent in his curiosity abut his mother's dual nature. See also Francis X. Charet, "Spiritualism and the Foundations of

C. G. Jung's Psychology," doctoral dissertation, University of Ottawa (June 1989).

34. Brome relates an anecdote about a patient named Babette whom Freud found repulsive and Jung found "fascinating" (Brome, *Jung,* p. 108).

35. See also Ellenberger, *The Discovery of the Unconscious,* p. 662.

36. Winnicott suggests that Jung's autobiography illuminates psychotic mental processes rather than neurotic ones ("Review," pp. 450–51).

37. Nini Herman, *My Kleinian Home: A Journey through Four Psychotherapies* (London: Quartet Books, 1985), p. 71.

38. Ibid., p. 74.

39. Ibid., p. 65.

40. Ibid., p. 64.

41. Ibid., p. 63.

42. "No word is metaphysical without its first being physical," Norman O. Brown, *Love's Body* (New York: Vintage Books, 1966), p. 249. See also Ella Sharpe, "Psycho-Physical Problems Revealed in Language: An Examination of Metaphor," in *Collected Papers on Psycho-Analysis,* ed. Marjorie Brierley (London: Hogarth Press, 1970), p. 156.

Chapter 9

This essay was originally presented as a talk at the panel on feminist theory and religion at the meeting of the American Academy of Religion in Atlanta, Georgia, in November 1986.

1. Shulamith Firestone, *The Dialectic of Sex: The Case for Feminist Revolution* (New York: Bantam Books, 1971), p. 44.

2. Joy Kogawa, "Snow White Meets the Mirror on the Wall," unpublished manuscript.

3. In his early work, Freud links psychic trauma to unconscious memories which remain cut off from thoughts and memories. At times, he says that cure erodes the symptom through conscious psychical activity.

Incidentally, a healthy psychical mechanism has other methods of dealing with the affect of a psychical trauma even if motor reaction and reaction by words are denied to it—namely by working it over associatively and by producing contrasting ideas. . . . Whether a healthy man deals with an insult in one way or the other, he always succeeds in achieving the result that the affect which was originally strong in his memory eventually loses intensity and that finally the recollection, having lost its affect, falls a victim to forgetfulness and the process of wearing-away. (Sigmund Freud, *The Standard Edition of the Complete Psychological Works of Sigmund Freud,* ed. James Strachey, 24 vols. [London: Hogarth Press, 1953–74], 3:37)

4. Nelle Morton, *The Journey Is Home* (Boston: Beacon Press, 1985).
5. Elisabeth Schüssler-Fiorenza writes about how the Bible has been made into a fetish. She wants to see scripture treated as "bread not stone." See Schüssler-Fiorenza, *In Memory of Her: A Feminist Reconstruction of Christian Origins* (New York: Crossroad, 1983), and *Bread, Not Stone: The Challenge of Feminist Biblical Interpretation* (Boston: Beacon Press, 1984).
6. Marie Cardinal, *The Words to Say It,* trans. Pat Goodheart (Cambridge, Mass.: VanVactor and Goodheart, 1983), pp. 239–40.
7. Freud, *Standard Edition,* 22:80.
8. Bruno Bettelheim, *Freud and Man's Soul* (New York: Alfred A. Knopf, 1983). The particular phrase has been used by Dr. W. Ann Mully, a Kleinian psychoanalyst practicing in Ottawa.
9. "The discourses of mastery" is a phrase used by Hélène Cixous and Catherine Clément, *The Newly Born Woman,* trans. Betsy Wing (Minneapolis. University of Minnesota Press, 1986).
10. Alison M. Jaggar and William L. McBride, "Reproduction as Male Ideology," *Women's Studies International Forum* 8, no. 3 (1985): 185–96.
11. Carol P. Christ, *The Laughter of Aphrodite: Reflections on a Journey to the Goddess* (San Francisco: Harper and Row, 1987).
12. Quoted by Phyllis Grosskurth, *Melanie Klein: Her World and Her Work* (Toronto: McClelland and Stewart, 1986), pp. 244–45.
13. Audre Lorde, *Sister/Outsider* (Trumansburg, N.Y.: Crossing Press, 1984), p. 147.
14. bell hooks, *Feminist Theory from Margin to Center* (Boston: South End Press, 1984).

Chapter 10

1. Mary Daly, *Pure Lust: Elemental Feminist Philosophy* (Boston: Beacon Press, 1984).
2. For a book which sets Klein's theories in the context of her life, see Phyllis Grosskurth's, *Melanie Klein: Her World and Her Work* (Toronto: McClelland and Stewart, 1986).

3. Norman O. Brown, *Life against Death* (New York: Random House, 1959), pp. 26–27.

4. Melanie Klein, "The Importance of Symbol Formation in the Development of the Ego," in *Love, Guilt, and Reparation and Other Works, 1921–1945* (New York: Delacorte Press, 1975), pp. 219–32.

5. Melanie Klein, "The Emotional Life of the Infant," in *Envy and Gratitude and Other Works, 1946–1963* (New York: Delacorte Press, 1975), p. 73.

6. Ibid., p. 74.

7. Ibid., p. 83.

8. Klein's theory about the sense of anger and persecution which drives the human mind to imagine the body in pieces can be applied to feminist analysis of advertising and pornography. According to her theory, images that dwell on parts of the body are angry images. They reveal an anger in the creator of the image, and their popularity indicates anger in those who consume them. Perhaps the images even foment rage in an audience by mirroring the fragmentation that fear inspires in the psyche. The concept may prove useful in understanding the structure of violent fantasies and in evaluating their effects.

9. Melitta Schmideberg, "The Role of Psychotic Mechanisms in Cultural Development," *International Journal of Psycho-Analysis* 11 (1930): 387–418.

10. Ibid., p. 404.

11. Ibid., p. 406.

12. See, for example, James Hillman, *Revisioning Psychology* (New York: Harper and Row, 1975).

13. Melanie Klein, *The Psycho-Analysis of Children,* trans. Alix Strachey (New York: Dell Publishing Co., 1975), p. 171. See also "Archetypal Theory and the Separation of Mind and Body: Reason Enough to Turn to Freud?" chapter 5 in this volume.

14. Marina Warner, *Alone of All Her Sex: The Myth and Cult of the Virgin Mary* (New York: Alfred A. Knopf, 1976), p. 204.

15. Philip E. Slater, *The Glory of Hera* (Boston: Beacon Press, 1968), p. 29.

16. "To Demeter," in *Hesiod: The Homeric Hymns and Homerica,* trans. Hugh G. Evelyn-White (Cambridge: Harvard University Press, 1970), pp. 306–7, lines 248–49.

17. "To Demeter", pp. 288–89, line 4.

18. C. G. Jung, *Answer to Job,* in *The Collected Works of C. G. Jung,* ed. William McGuire et al., trans. R. F. C. Hull, Bollingen Series 20. (Princeton:

Princeton University Press, 1969), 11, pp. 410–11. For an explanation of how Jung's own fear of his father may have contributed to his insight into Christ's feelings of ambivalence, see "Looking at Jung Looking at Himself: A Psychoanalytic Rereading of *Memories, Dreams, Reflections,*" chapter 8 in this volume.

19. Jung, *Answer to Job*, p. 408.

20. In contrast to Christianity's image of an all-perfect deity, Judaism's picture of God is more ambivalent. A number of passages in rabbinic literature reveal that the sages had mixed feelings toward a God who allowed the Jewish people to experience so much suffering ("R. Pinhas said: Moses established the form of prayer—'the great, mighty, and wonderful God' [Deut. 10:17]. Jeremiah said 'the great and mighty God,' [32:18] but did not say 'wonderful.' Why did he say 'mighty'? It is appropriate to call Him mighty if He watches the destruction of his Temple and remains silent . . . Daniel said 'the great and wonderful God,' [9:4] but did not say 'mighty.' If His children are enslaved, where is his might? [TR Berakhot 7.3 11c]." I am grateful to Judith Plaskow for drawing my attention to this ambivalence and to the above passages, which she cited in a letter to me.) This Jewish suspicion of God is, in my opinion, a sane attitude, which could form the basis for some useful theological reflection on the dynamics of human aggression. Nevertheless, I feel that idealization generated by the concept of God presents a problem for Judaism as well as for Christianity. In Judaism, it is the Jewish people who tend to be idealized. We Jews, I fear, sometimes are taught to see ourselves as people who are set apart from the rest of the world because of our special relationship to God, whether he is good or bad. It is the theological idea of being God's chosen people, which, in my view, promotes both an idealization of what it means to be Jewish and a tendency to look down on the gentile world. Although I understand and even excuse the Jewish sense of specialness as a psychological reaction which gives comfort for the agonies of persecution, I still feel that it needs to be confronted. We Jews should consider that the idealization of being Jewish may promote an exclusiveness in Jewish communities and may sometimes justify a lack of concern for the problems of other ethnic groups such as Arabs and blacks. Further, I think that we ought to be suspicious of how the idealization of a Jewish homeland may be functioning to inhibit criticism of Israel on the part of many Jews. A Jewish homeland is necessary, yes. But support for the existence of Israel should not preclude recognition of the mistakes of the Israeli government. The idea of chosenness deserves to be questioned because it inhibits some necessary critiques of contemporary Jewish politics.

21. Melanie Klein, "The Early Development of Conscience in the Child," in *Love, Guilt, and Reparation*, p. 257.

22. Carol Gilligan, *In a Different Voice* (Cambridge: Harvard University Press, 1982).

Chapter 11

1. Hans Küng, *Does God Exist?* trans. Edward Quinn (Garden City: Doubleday and Co., 1980), p. 301.

2. Ibid., p. 333.

3. Ibid., p. 329.

4. Paul Ricoeur, *Freud and Philosophy: An Essay on Interpretation*, trans. Denis Savage (New Haven: Yale University Press, 1970), p. 530.

5. Ibid., p. 531.

6. Peter Homans, *Theology after Freud* (New York: Bobbs-Merrill Co., 1970), p. 222.

7. Ibid., p. 326.

8. Duality in religious traditions is, I think, linked to idealization. See chapter 10, note 20, in this volume.

9. D. H. Lawrence, *Fantasia of the Unconscious* (Middlesex: Penguin Books, 1971), p. 12.

10. Sigmund Freud, *The Standard Edition of the Complete Psychological Works of Sigmund Freud*, ed. James Strachey, 24 vols. (London: Hogarth Press, 1953–74), 2:7.

11. Ibid., pp. 11–17.

12. Dianne Hunter, "Hysteria, Psychoanalysis, and Feminism: The Case of Anna O," *Feminist Studies*, Fall 1983, p. 486.

13. Freud, *Standard Edition*, 14:78.

14. Ibid., 23:158.

15. Charles Rycroft, *Imagination and Reality* (New York: International Universities Press, 1968), p. 58.

16. Freud, *Standard Edition*, 14:204.

17. Ricoeur, *Freud and Philosophy*, p. 544.

18. Freud, *Standard Edition*, 20:247.

19. Sigmund Freud and Oskar Pfister, *The Letters of Sigmund Freud and Oskar Pfister*, ed. Heinrich Meng and Ernst L. Freud, trans. Eric Mosbacher (London: Hogarth Press and the Institute of Psycho-Analysis, 1963), p. 132.

20. Ernest Jones, *Psycho-Myth, Psycho-History* (New York: Stonehill Publishing Co., 1974), 2:237.

21. Ernest Jones, as quoted by D. W. Winnicott in "Mind and Its Relation to the Psyche-Soma," in his *Through Paediatrics to Psycho-Analysis* (London: Hogarth Press and the Institute of Psycho-Analysis, 1978), p. 243.

22. Winnicott, "Mind and Its Relation to the Psyche-Soma," p. 243. See also "Body and Psyche in the Work of James Hillman" and "Archetypal Theory and the Separation of Mind and Body: Reason Enough to Turn to Freud?" chapters 5 and 7 in this volume.

23. Rycroft, *Imagination and Reality,* p. 109.

24. Ibid., p. 111.

25. Ibid., p. 108.

26. Ibid., p. 105.

27. Ortega y Gasset as quoted by Rycroft, ibid., p. 113.

28. Ibid.

29. Adrienne Rich, from "Two Songs," as quoted by Elizabeth V. Spelman, "Woman as Body: Ancient and Contemporary Views," *Feminist Studies* 8, no. 1 (Spring 1982): 109.

30. Shulamith Firestone, *The Dialectic of Sex: The Case for Feminist Revolution* (New York: Bantam Books, 1971), p. 44. See also "The Same Stuff: The Talking Cure of Feminism and Psychoanalysis," chapter 9 in this volume.

31. Freud, *Standard Edition,* 1: 179.

32. Ibid., 19: 257–58.

33. See "Anger in the Body: The Impact of Idealization on Human Development and Religion," chapter 10 in this volume.

34. For insight into this, see John E. Toews, "Male and Female Perspectives on a Psychoanalytic Myth," in *Gender and Religion: On the Complexity of Symbols,* ed. Caroline Walker Bynum, Stevan Harrell, and Paula Richman (Boston: Beacon Press, 1986), pp. 289–317.

35. "What will [women] write that is new?" Julia Kristeva, "Women's Time," trans. Alice Jardine and Harry Blake, in *Signs* 7, no. 1 (Autumn 1981): 32.

Chapter 12

1. This five-part *Ideas* series, written and narrated by Merlin Stone, was first aired in February 1986. The modern Goddess movement was surveyed from the time of the publication of Stone's book, *When God Was a Woman* (New York: Dial Press, 1976), to the present.

2. For example, see Z. Budapest, *The Holy Book of Women's Mysteries,* 2

vols. (Oakland: Susan B. Anthony Coven No. 1, 1979) and *The Grand-mothers of Time: A Woman's Book of Spells, Celebrations, and Sacred Objects for Every Month of the Year* (San Francisco: Harper and Row, 1989), and Starhawk, *The Spiral Dance: A Rebirth of the Ancient Religion of the Great Goddess* (San Francisco: Harper and Row, 1979).

3. See Carl Olsen, ed., *The Book of the Goddess: Past and Present* (New York: Crossroad, 1983).

4. See, for example, a discussion of the Goddess with reference to psychology in Jean Shinoda Bolen, *The Goddesses in Everywoman* (Los Angeles: J. P. Tarcher, 1982), and in Christine Downing, *The Goddess: Mythological Representations of the Feminine* (New York: Crossroad, 1984); to literature in E. M. Broner, *A Weave of Women* (New York: Holt, Rinehart and Winston, 1978; Bantam Books, 1980); to art in Judy Chicago, *The Dinner Party: A Symbol of Our Heritage* (Garden City: Doubleday, 1979); to history in Stone, *When God Was a Woman;* and to theological thought in Carol Christ, *Laughter of Aphrodite: Reflections on a Journey to the Goddess* (New York: Harper and Row, 1987), and in Judith Plaskow and Carol Christ, eds. *Weaving the Visions: New Patterns in Feminist Spirituality* (New York: Harper and Row, 1989).

5. *Thealogy,* the *logos* of *thea,* the Goddess, is surely a more appropriate term to refer to this new religion than is the word *theology,* which denotes an exclusively male God, *theos.* See Emily Erwin Culpepper, "Contemporary Goddess Thealogy: A Sympathetic Critique," in *Shaping New Visions: Gender and Values in American Culture,* ed. Clarissa W. Atkinson, Constance H. Buchanan, and Margaret R. Miles (Ann Arbor: UMI Research Press, 1987).

6. Melanie Klein, *Love, Guilt, and Reparation and Other Works, 1921–1945* (New York: Delacorte Press, 1975), and *Envy and Gratitude and Other Works, 1946–1963* (New York: Delacorte Press, 1975); W. Ronald D. Fairbairn, *Psychoanalytic Studies of the Personality* (London: Routledge and Kegan Paul, 1966); D. W. Winnicott, *Through Paediatrics to Psycho-Analysis* (London: Hogarth Press and the Institute of Psycho-Analysis, 1978), and *The Maturational Processes and the Facilitating Environment* (London: Hogarth Press and the Institute of Psycho-Analysis, 1979); and Michael Balint, *The Basic Fault* (London: Tavistock Publications, 1958).

7. Jay R. Greenberg and Stephen A. Mitchell, *Object Relations in Psychoanalytic Theory* (Boston: Harvard University Press, 1983).

8. Mircea Eliade, *Cosmos and History: The Myth of the Eternal Return,* trans. William R. Trask (New York: Harper and Row, 1959).

9. Sigmund Freud, *The Standard Edition of the Complete Psychological Works of Sigmund Freud,* ed. James Strachey, 24 vols. (London: Hogarth Press, 1953–74), 7:222.

10. For an account of how the images of witch and sorceress can be used to imagine new behavior in this world, see Hélène Cixous and Catherine Clément, *The Newly Born Woman,* trans. Betsy Wing (Minneapolis: University of Minnesota Press, 1986).

11. Stone, *When God Was a Woman*; Marija Gimbutas, *The Language of the Goddess* (San Francisco: Harper and Row, 1989); Savina Teubal, *Sarah the Priestess* (Cleveland: University of Ohio Press, 1984); and Charlene Spretnak, *Lost Goddesses of Early Greece: A Collection of Pre-Hellenic Myths* (Boston: Beacon Press, 1981).

12. Although his book is not about Goddess religion per se, Sherwin T. Wine's *Judaism Beyond God* (Farmington Hills, Mich.: Society for Humanistic Judaism, 1985) provides a good summary of important feminist ideas about patriarchal religious holidays. See especially pp. 151–78.

13. See, for example, the passage in Luke 11:27,28. It is interesting to contrast the various translations of this passage: for example, the New English Bible translation says: "While [Jesus] was speaking thus, a woman in the crowd called out, 'Happy the womb that carried you and the breasts that suckled you!' He rejoined, 'No, happy are those who hear the word of God and keep it.'" See also Rosemary Ruether, *New Woman/New Earth: Sexist Ideologies and Human Liberation* (New York: Seabury Press, 1975), p. 59.

14. Elisabeth Schüssler-Fiorenza, *In Memory of Her: A Feminist Theological Reconstruction of Christian Origins* (New York: Crossroad, 1983). Schüssler-Fiorenza believes that a feminist reconstruction of Christian beginnings is essential to empower women in their struggle against patriarchal oppression (p. xx). She thinks that concentrating on the apostolic tradition obscures the contributions of women to the early Church (p. 69). As an example of how this patriarchal version of history can be supplemented to include women, see her chapter entitled "The Early Christian Missionary Movement—Equality in the Power of the Spirit," pp. 160–204.

15. Luke 1:38. See also Marina Warner, *Alone of All Her Sex: The Myth and Cult of the Virgin Mary* (New York: Alfred A. Knopf, 1976). Warner argues that the image and iconography of Mary subsumes that of several goddesses in the Graeco-Roman pantheon—for example, Artemis (p. 280), Aphrodite (p. 279), Athene (p. 304), Hera (p. 267), and Persephone (p. 273).

16. Bruno Bettelheim, *Symbolic Wounds, Puberty Rites, and the Envious Male* (New York: Collier Books, 1962).

17. Mary Gendler, "The Restoration of Vashti," in *The Jewish Woman,* ed. Elizabeth Koltun (New York: Schocken Books, 1976), pp. 241–47. And see any issue of *Lilith: A Quarterly Magazine* (New York: Lilith Publications).

18. Klein, "Development of a Child," in *Love, Guilt, and Reparation,* p. 48.

19. Klein, "Envy and Gratitude," in *Envy and Gratitude,* p. 199.

20. Luce Irigaray, *The Speculum of the Other Woman,* trans. Gillian Gill (Ithaca: Cornell University Press, 1985), and *This Sex Which Is Not One,* trans. Catherine Porter (Ithaca: Cornell University Press, 1985).

21. As quoted in Greenberg and Mitchell, *Object Relations in Psychoanalytic Theory,* p. 197.

22. Margaret Mahler, "Ego Psychology Applied to Behavior Problems," in *Modern Trends in Child Psychiatry,* ed. N. D. C. Lewis and B. L. Pacella (New York: International Universities Press, 1946), as quoted in Greenberg and Mitchell, *Object Relations in Psychoanalytic Theory,* p. 282.

23. Joan Riviere, "The Unconscious Phantasy of an Inner World Reflected in Examples from Literature," in *New Directions in Psychoanalysis,* ed. M. Klein (New York: Basic Books, 1955), pp. 358–59, as quoted in Norman O. Brown, *Love's Body* (New York: Random House, 1966), p. 147.

24. See essays in Sandra Harding and Merrill B. Hintikka, eds., *Discovering Reality: Feminist Perspectives on Epistemology, Metaphysics, Methodology, and Philosophy of Science* (Dordrecht: D. Reidel, 1983).

25. Naomi Schemen, "Individualism and the Objects of Psychology," in Harding and Hintikka, *Discovering Reality,* pp. 225–44.

26. Starhawk, "Ethics and Justice in Goddess Religion," in *The Politics of Women's Spirituality: Essays on the Rise of Spiritual Power within the Feminist Movement* (New York: Doubleday, 1982), p. 418.

27. Ibid., pp. 415–16.

28. Object relations theorists use "phantasy" to refer to unconscious "fantasy." "Fantasy" is given various interpretations and definitions in psychoanalytic literature. I am using the term broadly to refer in a general way to imagination, imaging, and so forth.

29. See Charles Rycroft, "Symbolism and Its Relationship to the Primary and Secondary Processes," in *Imagination and Reality* (New York: International Universities Press, 1968), pp. 42–60, and Susan Isaacs, "The Nature

and Function of Phantasy," *International Journal of Psycho-Analysis* 29 (1948): 73–97. Freud's attitude toward so-called fantasy thinking is discussed extensively by Judith Van Herik in *Freud on Femininity and Faith* (Berkeley: University of California Press, 1982).

30. On the contrary, psychoanalysis sees willpower as playing a role in the *repression* of fantasy.

31. Paula Heimann, "Certain Functions of Introjection and Projection in Early Infancy," in *Developments in Psycho-Analysis,* ed. Susan Isaacs, Melanie Klein, and Jean Riviere (London: Hogarth Press, 1952), pp. 122–68, as quoted in Phyllis Grosskurth, *Melanie Klein: Her World and Her Work* (Toronto: McClelland and Stewart, 1986), p. 331.

32. See, for example, "Archetypal Theory and the Separation of Mind and Body: Reason Enough to Turn to Freud?" chapter 5 in this volume.

33.

Enuma Elish, iv. 101
He shot therethrough an arrow, it pierced her stomach,
Clave through her bowels, tore into her womb:
Thereat he strangled her, made her life-breath ebb away,
Cast her body to the ground, standing over it [in triumph].

135
He rested, the lord, examining her body:
Would divide up the monster, create a wonder of wonders!
He slit her in two like a fish of the drying yards,
The one half he positioned and secured as the sky . . .

vi. 1
[Therein] traced he lines for the mighty gods,
Stars, star-groups and constellations he appointed for them:
He determined the year, marked out its divisions,
For each of the twelve months appointed three rising stars.

5
Having established the rules for the [astronomical] seasons,
He laid down the Crossing-line to make known their limits:
And that none should make mistake or in any way lose speed
He appointed, conjointly with in, the Enlil—and Ea—lines.

9
The great [Sun-]gates he opened in both sides of her ribs,
Made strong the lock-fastening to left and right:

In the depths of her belly he laid down the *elati*.
He made the moon to shine forth, entrusted to him the night.

53
He placed her in position, heaped [the mountai]ns upon it . . .
Made the Euphr[ates] and Tigris to flow through her eyes.

(From "The Epic of Creation," in *Documents from Old Testament Times,* ed. and trans. D. Winton Thomas (New York: Harper and Row, 1958), pp. 10–11.)
34. See "Anger in the Body: The Impact of Idealization on Human Development and Religion," chapter 10 of this volume.
35. Winnicott, "Transitional Objects and Transitional Phenomena," in *Through Paedriatrics to Psycho-Analysis,* pp. 229–42.
36. W. R. Bion, "A Way of Thinking," in *Second Thoughts: Selected Papers on Psycho-Analysis* (New York: Jason Aronson, 1967), pp. 110–19.

Conclusion

1. *Webster's New World Dictionary, College Edition* (Cleveland and New York: World Publishing Co., 1955), p. 1406.
2. Ibid.

Bibliography

Atkinson, Clarissa W., Constance H. Buchanan, and Margaret R. Miles, eds. *Shaping New Visions: Gender and Values in American Culture.* Ann Arbor, UMI Research Press, 1987.

Atwood, Margaret. *You Are Happy.* Toronto: Oxford University Press, 1974.

Balint, Michael. *The Basic Fault.* London: Tavistock Publications, 1958.

Barthes, Roland. *Mythologies.* Translated and edited by Annette Lavers. New York: Hill and Wang, 1972.

Becker, Ernest. *The Denial of Death.* New York: Free Press, Macmillan Publishing Co., 1973.

Bettelheim, Bruno. *Freud and Man's Soul.* New York: Alfred A. Knopf, 1983.

——. *Symbolic Wounds, Puberty Rites, and the Envious Male.* New York: Collier Books, 1962.

Bion, W. R. *Second Thoughts: Selected Papers on Psycho-Analysis.* New York: Jason Aronson, 1967.

Bolen, Jean Shinoda. *The Goddesses in Everywoman.* Los Angeles: J. P. Tarcher, 1982.

Broner, E. M. *A Weave of Women.* New York: Holt, Rinehart and Winston, 1978; Bantam Books, 1980.

Brown, Norman O. *Closing Time.* New York: Random House, 1973.

——. *Life against Death: The Psychoanalytical Meaning of History.* New York: Random House, 1959.

——. *Love's Body.* New York: Random House, 1966.

Budapest, Z. *The Grandmothers of Time: A Woman's Book of Spells, Celebrations, and Sacred Objects for Every Month of the Year.* San Francisco: Harper and Row, 1989.

——. *The Holy Book of Women's Mysteries.* 2 vols. Oakland: Susan B. Anthony Coven No. 1, 1979.

Bynum, Caroline Walker, Stevan Harrell, and Paula Richman, eds. *Gender and Religion: On the Complexity of Symbols.* Boston: Beacon Press, 1986.

Cardinal, Marie. *The Words to Say It.* Translated by Pat Goodheart. Cambridge, Mass.: VanVactor and Goodheart, 1983.

Charet, Francis X. "Spiritualism and the Foundations of C. G. Jung's Psychology." Doctoral dissertation. University of Ottawa: June, 1989.

Chicago, Judy. *The Dinner Party: A Symbol of Our Heritage.* Garden City: Doubleday, 1979.

Chodorow, Nancy. *Feminism and Psychoanalytic Theory.* New Haven: Yale University Press, 1989.

———. *The Reproduction of Mothering.* Berkeley: University of California Press, 1978.

Christ, Carol P. *Diving Deep and Surfacing: Women Writers on Spiritual Quest,* 2d ed. Boston: Beacon Press, 1986.

———. *Laughter of Aphrodite: Reflections on a Journey to the Goddess.* New York: Harper and Row, 1987.

Cixous, Hélène and Catherine Clément. *The Newly Born Woman.* Trans. Betsy Wing. Minneapolis: University of Minnesota Press, 1986.

Culpepper, Emily Erwin. "Contemporary Goddess Thealogy: A Sympathetic Critique." In *Shaping New Vision: Gender and Values in American Culture,* edited by Clarissa W. Atkinson, Constance H. Buchanan, and Margaret R. Miles. Ann Arbor: UMI Research Press, 1987.

Daly, Herman E., and John B. Cobb, Jr. *For the Common Good: Redirecting the Economy toward Community, the Environment, and a Sustainable Future.* Boston: Beacon Press, 1989.

De Beauvoir, Simone. *The Second Sex.* Translated and edited by H. M. Parshley. New York: Alfred A. Knopf, 1952.

Deren, Maya. *Divine Horsemen: The Voodoo Gods of Haiti.* New York: Dell Publishing Co., 1970.

Dillard, Annie. *Pilgrim at Tinker Creek.* New York: Harper and Row, Perennial Library, 1985 (1974).

Dinnerstein, Dorothy. *The Mermaid and the Minotaur: Sexual Arrangements and Human Malaise.* New York: Harper and Row, 1976.

Dodson Gray, Elizabeth. *Why the Green Nigger?* Wellesley: Roundtable Press, 1979.

Downing, Christine. *The Goddess: Mythological Representations of the Feminine.* New York: Crossroad, 1984.

———. *Myths and Mysteries of Same-Sex Love.* New York: Continuum, 1989.

Eliade, Mircea. *Cosmos and History: The Myth of the Eternal Return.* Translated by William R. Trask. New York: Harper and Row, 1959.

242

Fairbairn, W. Ronald D. *Psychoanalytic Studies of the Personality*. London: Routledge and Kegan Paul, 1966.

Fawcett, Brian. *Cambodia: A Book for People Who Find Television Too Slow*. Vancouver: Talonbooks, 1986.

Finn, Geraldine. "Women and the Ideology of Science." *Our Generation* 15, no. 1.

———, ed. *Voices of Feminism: An Introduction to Feminism and Women's Studies*. Toronto: Garamond Press, 1990.

Finn, Geraldine, and Angela Miles, eds. *Feminism in Canada: From Pressure to Politics*. Montreal: Black Rose Books, 1983.

Firestone, Shulamith. *The Dialectic of Sex: The Case for Feminist Revolution*. New York: Bantam Books, 1971.

Flax, Jane. *Thinking Fragments: Psychoanalysis, Feminism, and Postmodernism in the Contemporary West*. Berkeley: University of California Press, 1990.

Freud, Sigmund. *The Standard Edition of the Complete Psychological Works of Sigmund Freud*. Edited by James Strachey. 24 vols. London: Hogarth Press, 1953–74.

Freud, Sigmund, and Oskar Pfister. *The Letters of Sigmund Freud and Oskar Pfister*. Edited by Heinrich Meng and Ernst L. Freud, translated by Eric Mosbacher. London: Hogarth Press and the Institute of Psycho-Analysis, 1963.

Gadon, Elinor. *The Once and Future Goddess*. New York: Harper and Row, 1989.

Gallop, Jane. *The Daughter's Seduction: Feminism and Psychoanalysis*. Ithaca. Cornell University Press, 1982.

———. *Thinking Through the Body*. New York: Columbia University Press, 1988.

Gendler, Mary. "The Restoration of Vashti." In *The Jewish Woman*, edited by Elizabeth Koltun. New York: Schocken Books, 1976.

Gimbutas, Marija. *The Language of the Goddess*. San Francisco: Harper and Row, 1989.

Gitlin, Todd. "Postmodernism Defined, At Last!" *Utne Reader*, July/August 1989, pp. 52–61.

Goldenberg, Naomi R. "Archetypal Theory after Jung." In *Spring 1975*, pp. 199–220. Zürich: Spring Publications, 1975.

———. *Changing of the Gods: Feminism and the End of Traditional Religions*. Boston: Beacon Press, 1979.

———. "Feminism and Jungian Theory." *Anima* 3, no. 2 (Spring 1977): 14–17.

———. "A Feminist Critique of Jung." *Signs* 2, no. 2 (Winter 1976): 443–49.

Greenberg, Jay R., and Stephen A. Mitchell. *Object Relations in Psychoanalytic Theory.* Boston: Harvard University Press, 1983.

Griffin, Susan. *Women and Nature.* New York: Harper and Row, 1978.

Grosskurth, Phyllis. *Melanie Klein: Her World and Her Work.* Toronto: McClelland and Stewart, 1986.

Harding, Sandra, and Merrill B. Hintikka, eds. *Discovering Reality: Feminist Perspectives on Epistemology, Metaphysics, Methodology, and Philosophy of Science.* Dordrecht: D. Reidel, 1983.

Herald, Childe. "Freud and Football." In *Reader in Comparative Religion: An Anthropological Approach,* 2d ed., edited by William A. Lessa and Evon Z. Vogt, pp. 250–52. New York: Harper and Row, 1965.

Hillman, James. "*Anima Mundi:* The Return of the Soul to the World." In *Spring 1982,* pp. 71–93. Dallas: Spring Publications, 1982.

———. *Archetypal Psychology: A Brief Account.* Dallas: Spring Publications, 1983.

———. *A Blue Fire: Selected Writings by James Hillman.* Edited by Thomas Moore. New York: Harper and Row, 1989.

———. *Healing Fiction.* Tarrytown, N.Y.: Station Hill Press, 1983.

———. *Inter Views.* New York: Harper and Row, 1983.

———. *Revisioning Psychology.* New York: Harper and Row, 1975.

Homans, Peter. *Jung in Context: Modernity and the Making of a Psychology.* Chicago: University of Chicago Press, 1979.

———. *Theology after Freud.* New York: Bobbs-Merrill Co., 1970.

Hooks, Bell. *Feminist Theory from Margin to Center.* Boston: South End Press, 1984.

Hunter, Dianne. "Hysteria, Psychoanalysis, and Feminism: The Case of Anna O." *Feminist Studies* (Fall 1983).

Irigaray, Luce. *This Sex Which Is Not One.* Translated by Catherine Porter. Ithaca: Cornell University Press, 1985.

———. *The Speculum of the Other Woman.* Translated by Gillian Gill. Ithaca: Cornell University Press, 1985.

Isaacs, Susan. "The Nature and Function of Phantasy." *International Journal of Psycho-Analysis* 29 (1948): 73–97.

Jacoby, Russell. *The Last Intellectuals: American Culture in the Age of Academe.* New York: Basic Books, 1987.

Jaggar, Alison M., and William L. McBride. "Reproduction as Male Ideology." *Women's Studies International Forum* 8, no. 3 (1985): 185–96.

Jones, Ernest. *Psycho-Myth, Psycho-History*. 2 vols. New York: Stonehill Publishing Co., 1974.

Jung, C. G. *The Collected Works of C. G. Jung*. Edited by William G. McGuire et al., translated by R. F. C. Hull. Bollingen Series 20. 20 vols. Princeton: Princeton University Press, 1954–79.

———. *C. G. Jung Speaking: Interviews and Encounters*. Edited by William McGuire and R. F. C. Hull. Princeton: Princeton University Press, 1977.

———. *Memories, Dreams, Reflections*. New York: Random House, 1961.

Keller, Catherine. *From a Broken Web: Separation, Sexism, and the Self*. Boston: Beacon Press, 1986.

Keller, Evelyn Fox. *A Feeling for the Organism: The Life and Work of Barbara McClintock*. New York: Freeman, 1983.

———. *Reflections on Gender and Science*. New Haven: Yale University Press, 1985.

Khan, Masud. *Alienation in Perversion*. New York: International Universities Press, 1979.

Klein, Melanie. *Envy and Gratitude and Other Works, 1946–1963*. New York: Delacorte Press, 1975.

———. *Love, Guilt, and Reparation and Other Works, 1921–1945*. New York: Delacorte Press, 1975.

Koltun, Elizabeth, ed. *The Jewish Woman*. New York: Schocken Books, 1976.

Kristeva, Julia. *Desire in Language*. Edited by Leon S. Roudiez. New York: Columbia University Press, 1980.

———. *The Kristeva Reader*. Translated by Leon S. Roudiez, edited by Toril Moi. New York: Columbia University Press, 1986.

———. "Women's Time." Translated by Alice Jardine and Harry Blake. *Signs* 7, no. 1 (Autumn 1981): 13–35.

Küng, Hans. *Does God Exist?* Translated by Edward Quinn. Garden City: Doubleday and Co., 1980.

Lauter, Estella, and Carol Schreier Rupprecht, eds. *Feminist Archetypal Theory: Interdisciplinary Revisions of Jungian Thought*. Knoxville: University of Tennessee Press, 1985.

Lawrence, D. H. *Fantasia of the Unconscious*. Middlesex: Penguin Books, 1971.

Lorde, Audre. *Sister/Outsider*. Trumansburg, N.Y.: Crossing Press, 1984.

Malcolm, Janet. "The Psychoanalyst Plays Polo: Review of *The Long Wait and Other Psychoanalytic Narratives*, by Masud R. Khan." *New York Times Book Review*, April 9, 1989.

Marks, Elaine, and Isabelle de Courtivron, eds. *New French Feminisms: An Anthology*. New York: Schocken Books, 1981.

Morton, Nelle. *The Journey Is Home*. Boston: Beacon Press, 1985.

Newson, Janice, and Howard Buchbinder. *The University Means Business*. Toronto: Garamond Press, 1988.

O'Brien, Mary. *The Politics of Reproduction*. London: Routledge and Kegan Paul, 1981.

Olsen, Carl, ed. *The Book of the Goddess: Past and Present*. New York: Crossroad, 1983.

Plaskow, Judith, and Carol Christ, eds. *Weaving the Visions: New Patterns in Feminist Spirituality*. New York: Harper and Row, 1989.

Plato. *The Collected Dialogues of Plato*. Edited by Edith Hamilton and Huntington Cairns. New York: Pantheon, 1966.

Rich, Adrienne. *Of Woman Born*. New York: Bantam Books, 1976.

Ricoeur, Paul. *Freud and Philosophy: An Essay on Interpretation*. Translated by Denis Savage. New Haven: Yale University Press, 1970.

Robbins, Tom. *Still Life with Woodpecker*. New York: Bantam Books, 1980.

Ruether, Rosemary. *New Woman/New Earth: Sexist Ideologies and Human Liberation*. New York: Seabury Press, 1975.

Rycroft, Charles. *Imagination and Reality*. New York: International Universities Press, 1968.

Schacochis, Bob. "In Deepest Gringolandia—Mexico: The Third World as Tourist Theme Park." *Harper's* 279, no. 1670 (July 1989): 42–50.

Schemen, Naomi. "Individualism and the Objects of Psychology." In *Discovering Reality: Feminist Perspectives on Epistemology, Metaphysics, and Philosophy of Science,* edited by Sandra Harding and Merrill B. Hintikka, pp. 225–44. Dordrecht: D. Reidel, 1983.

Schüssler-Fiorenza, Elisabeth. *Bread, Not Stone: The Challenge of Feminist Biblical Interpretation*. Boston: Beacon Press, 1984.

——. *In Memory of Her: A Feminist Theological Reconstruction of Christian Origins*. New York: Crossroad, 1983.

Sharpe, Ella Freeman. *Collected Papers on Psycho-Analysis*. New York: Brunner/Mazel, 1978.

Sontag, Susan. *Against Interpretation*. New York: Dell Publishing Co., 1961.

——. *On Photography*. New York: Farrar, Straus and Giroux, 1978.

Spelman, Elizabeth V. "Woman as Body: Ancient and Contemporary Views." *Feminist Studies* 8, no. 1 (Spring 1982): 109–31.

Spretnak, Charlene. *Lost Goddesses of Early Greece: A Collection of Pre-Hellenic Myths*. Boston: Beacon Press, 1981.

———, ed. *The Politics of Women's Spirituality: Essays on the Rise of Spiritual Power within the Feminist Movement.* New York: Doubleday, 1982.

Starhawk. *Dreaming the Dark: Magic, Sex, and Politics.* Boston: Beacon Press, 1982.

———. *The Spiral Dance: A Rebirth of the Ancient Religion of the Great Goddess.* San Francisco: Harper and Row, 1979.

———. *Truth or Dare.* San Francisco: Harper and Row, 1987.

Stokes, Adrian. *Reflections on the Nude.* London: Tavistock Publications, 1967.

Stone, Merlin. *When God Was a Woman.* New York: Dial Press, 1976.

Teubal, Savina. *Sarah the Priestess.* Cleveland: University of Ohio Press, 1984.

Thomas, D. Winton, trans. and ed. *Documents from Old Testament Times.* New York: Harper and Row, 1958.

Toews, John E. "Male and Female Perspectives on a Psychoanalytic Myth." In *Gender and Religion: On the Complexity of Symbols,* edited by Caroline Walker Bynum, Stevan Harrell, and Paula Richman, pp. 289–317. Boston: Beacon Press, 1986.

Turkle, Sherry. *The Second Self: Computers and the Human Spirit.* New York: Simon and Schuster, 1984.

Van Herik, Judith. *Freud on Femininity and Faith.* Berkeley: University of California Press, 1982.

Warner, Marina. *Alone of All Her Sex: The Myth and Cult of the Virgin Mary.* New York: Alfred A. Knopf, 1976.

White, Lynne. "The Religious Roots of Our Ecological Crisis." *Science* 155 (1967): 1203–7.

Wine, Sherwin T. *Judaism Beyond God.* Farmington Hills, Mich.: Society for Humanistic Judaism, 1985.

Winnicott, D. W. *The Maturational Processes and the Facilitating Environment.* London: Hogarth Press and the Institute of Psycho-Analysis, 1979.

———. *Playing and Reality.* New York: Penguin Books, 1971.

———. *Through Paediatrics to Psycho-Analysis.* London: Hogarth Press and the Institute of Psycho-Analysis, 1978.

Index

249

Credits

Portions of this book have previously appeared in *Anima; Journal of Feminist Studies in Religion; Studies in Religion/Sciences Religieuses; Knowing Religiously*, ed. Leroy S. Rouner (Notre Dame, Indiana: University of Notre Dame Press, 1985); *Weaving the Visions: New Patterns in Feminist Spirituality*, ed. Judith Plaskow and Carol P. Christ (New York: Harper and Row, 1989); *Women and Men: Interdisciplinary Readings on Gender*, ed. Greta Hofmann Nemiroff (Toronto: Fitzhenry and Whiteside, 1987); *Religious Traditions and the Limits of Tolerance*, ed. Louis J. Hammann and Harry M. Buck (Chambersburg, Pa.: Anima Publications, 1988); *Feministische Theologie: Perspektiven zur Orientierung*, ed. Maria Kassel (Stuttgart: Kreuz Verlag, 1988); and *Souffles de femmes: Lectures féministes de la religion*, ed. Monique Dumais et Marie-Andrée Roy (Montréal et Paris: Les Éditions Paulines et Médiaspaul, 1989).

Grateful acknowledgment is made to Joy Kogawa for permission to quote from her manuscript "Snow White Meets the Mirror on the Wall."